P9-EDU-894

Pacific Pilgrims

Pacific Pilgrims

Lyndon Grove

Foreword by Godfrey P. Gower

FFORBEZ PUBLICATIONS LTD.
Box 35340
Vancouver, British Columbia

This book was prepared by Fforbez Publications on behalf of
the Centennial Committee
of the Anglican Diocese of New Westminster

Pacific Pilgrims

Editing, design, research assistance, photographic assistance, and selection and arrangement of pictorial materials by James R. Wright of Fforbez Publications.
Copies of halftones by John Versteeg of Custom Camera Reproductions Ltd.
Printed in Canada by National School Services Ltd.
Norm Shaw, Graphics Consultant.

Canadian Cataloguing in Publication Data

Grove, Lyndon, 1932-
Pacific Pilgrims

Includes index.
ISBN 0-88976-041-1
ISBN 0-88976-043-8 pa.

1. Anglican Church of Canada. Diocese of New Westminster — History — Pictorial works. 2. British Columbia — History — Pictorial works. I Anglican Church of Canada. Diocese of New Westminster. II. Title.
BX5612.N4G7 283'711'33 C79-091153-1

"Hallowed this dwelling"—Christ Church Cathedral, a spiritual oasis in downtown Vancouver.

Hallowed this dwelling where the Lord abideth,
This is none other than the gate of heaven;
Strangers and pilgrims, seeking homes eternal,
Pass through its portals.

–*The Book of Common Praise*

Cover: Columbia Coast Mission service at Sechelt Inlet in the Anglican Diocese of New Westminster. The photograph is reproduced from the cover of the Mission magazine *The Log*, November-December 1946.

Contents

Lyndon Grove, author of *Pacific Pilgrims*, and Archbishop Godfrey Gower, author of the foreword. Most Reverend Godfrey P. Gower, fifth Bishop of New Westminster, was consecrated in 1951 and installed as Metropolitan of the Province of British Columbia in 1968. After retiring in 1971, Archbishop Gower became Chancellor of Vancouver School of Theology in 1972.

Lyndon Grove, editor of the diocesan newspaper *Topic* and a prolific freelance writer, is known for his witty, erudite columns and broadcasts. Grove is a former editor of the *Vancouver Courier* and several other publications. He was creative director at CHQM, CKLG and Torresan Rose Marketing Communications and was co-author of the best-seller *Kids! Kids! Kids! and British Columbia.*

Foreword

Every surveyor knows that in charting a course he has to swing his instrument from the point from which he has come to the point ahead. With his ultimate destination in mind and with his knowledge of the terrain on which he stands, he transforms the uncharted way into a well-marked path over which others may travel.

Written history performs this function, and unless we cut ourselves off completely from the past we can derive much profit and pleasure in looking back.

It seems fairly obvious that the Church on its human side is in danger of losing its bearings. Many Christian landmarks have disappeared and in the welter of conflicting forces sweeping over the face of the globe we are in danger of losing our way.

Anniversaries – the celebration of accomplishments, events, and the commemoration of persons – are opportunities to survey the scene of action, to put the past, the present and the future together. In the Church, of all places, we ought to be able to say we know where we came from, we know where we are, and we know where we are going.

It is for this reason that we should keep our one hundredth anniversary as a diocese, reminding ourselves of the faith and witness of those who preceded us, and putting our own thoughts in true perspective as we look ahead.

It is altogether fitting that part of our celebration should be some account of a century of life in which the Church has grown up with a province of almost the same age. Not too much attention has been paid to the contribution of the Churches to the well-being of those who have settled here and become its citizens. In the early days conditions were harsh, amenities were few; racial tensions caused frequent bloodshed, law and order were difficult to maintain. It is not too much to say that, whatever criticisms were levelled at them, the Churches reminded the community of a morality and a character which added a refining grace and protected the decencies of human existence. This province is indebted to the Churches, our Anglican Church among them, for taking care of the Indians in the days when most thought of them as just savages to be exploited. The Churches pointed the way to education, establishing schools. The faithful amongst the laity, always the front line of Christian forces, became the conscience of society on many matters of right and justice.

The nineteenth century has been blamed for many things, and often the criticism is accompanied by such epithets as 'puritanical', 'hypocritical', 'narrow-minded'. Well! Perhaps. Those distortions are hardly more reprehensible than those we might, if we were so minded, apply censoriously to our present permissive society. What is of much more importance is to adjust and retain our perspective. Our diocese sprang out of the vision and the large-heartedness of men and women whose one purpose was to give the Gospel of our Lord and Saviour Jesus Christ a chance to work its own redeeming influence in the lives of men and women in a far-flung corner of the earth.

We may conjure up in our mind's eye that remarkable meeting in London attended by the Archbishop of Canterbury and other bishops, by the city fathers of the metropolis, by businessmen and members of parliament joining in an enthusiastic response to the appeal of the newly appointed bishop of British Columbia. We may think of the commanding officer of the Royal Engineers conducting Morning Prayer in the street in Yale in the presence of his soldiers, gold-miners, Indians and others. We may see Bishop Sillitoe sitting at the door of his tent playing the accompaniment to the hymns he was trying to teach his "Indian children". Nothing seems quite as incongruous as the self-portrait of that small-built missionary, the Rev. W.B. Crickmer, whose cartoons depict him as a thoroughly domesticated husband caring for the baby, and as a black-coated street evangelist standing on a barrel in the middle of the street trying to catch the attention of the men lounging on the wooden duckwalk outside the tavern. Does the upsweeping skyline of the mountain named after him give us a better impression of the spirit that animated him and all those others who followed him to bring the Gospel, to build the Church and to infuse into society those spiritual values which are the glue of a Christian civilization?

In any case we should be greatly remiss if we failed to acknowledge the great debt we owe to the Church of England, the vision of its leaders, the generosity of its laity, the dedication and courage of its missionaries, and the determination of her sons and daughters in a distant land to have their Churches in which they could worship and receive the comfort of its ministrations.

It saves us from parochialism to recall that what happened in British Columbia during the latter half of the nineteenth century was only a part of the Mother Church's magnificent effort to meet its missionary obligations. It is a facile criticism to say it followed the flag, or it was allied to empire strategy or that it was supported in its work by commercial interests. The fact remains that, irrespective of the conditions under which it laboured, such was the effectiveness of its policies and the coherence of its message that there emerged in the twentieth century a worldwide Church embracing in its membership many races, kindreds and tongues.

Of this fellowship, the Anglican Church of Canada is a healthy and vigorous member, and in that membership the diocese of New Westminster is playing a very important role.

We do well to remember, as the principal of the University College of the Gold Coast reminded the First Anglican Congress in Minneapolis in 1954, that our place in Christendom is a small one, and modesty becomes us better than inflated claims. Our Anglican Communion is only a tiny fraction of the total company of Christians on earth. We would be optimistic if we claimed to be five per cent and can only pray that under God our influence is not less in proportion.

No Church, large or small, can afford to indulge in self-praise or live in cloud-cuckoo land. This century is witnessing a fierce battle for the soul of mankind and the forces arrayed against the Christian Church are very powerful. It is not a matter of saving our skins. It is a matter of understanding the issues of the day and of knowing how to bring to bear upon them the principles and values that spring from Christian thinking.

When Archdeacon Pentreath, who in a very real sense was the architect of the diocesan structure, presented his fourteenth report to the twenty-ninth session of the Synod in 1911, he gave a vivid account of the growth and development that had taken place since his appointment. It was in effect an account of his stewardship and as he concluded he added a personal word. He pleaded for broadmindedness and greater charity. He urged the delegates, clergy and laity alike, not to let non-essentials and trifles dissipate the Church's energies. He ended with these words: "Give us men... men on fire with zeal for Christ and the Church, men in touch with the times in which they are living."

As I think of the changes and chances through which we have come in our first hundred years, that voice from the past still moves me deeply. I hear, too, the firm but kindly word of Bishop Sillitoe charting the course of a Church which was endangered by ritualistic controversies. Drawing the sting, he made it clear he would not be partisan and would respect every man's conviction—principle with tolerance, not intolerance over principle. Then too there comes to mind the admonition to the clergy by the scholarly Bishop Dart reminding some who had pressed their preferences in parish matters too forcibly that "the laity have their rights too".

Here we have the spirit and the mutual understanding which underguided the loyalty of the bishops, clergy and laity as they pressed forward in the common task. Some would have the Church move more quickly. A day in which instant responses and instant solutions are demanded is a time which finds our caution irritating. It is true we have more of the tortoise in our make-up than the hare. We seem, also, to like the idea that the Kingdom of God comes secretly and quickly, "in little things past the low lintel of the human heart", rather than in the dangerous explosiveness of the public crowd. We can be forgiven for drawing attention to the fact that in the story the end of the race was in favour of the tortoise.

As the diocese looks ahead we can be deeply grateful that we are privileged to take up the task left to us by those who responded to the call in the field of human need. The Church has been served by a faithful clergy and by a host of men and women who have loved it dearly. It has nothing to fear. It can draw on the great spiritual resources of the past and the experience of centuries in dealing with human nature. Whether the world thinks so or not it has a message for humanity. All we need to be concerned with is the proclamation by word and deed and loving care of that message so that hearts may find God.

In the month of August, 1881, Bishop Sillitoe embarked on a journey into the interior. Of the first part of the journey the bishop gives his own account.

"We should never have started had we listened to the gloomy vaticinations of anxious friends. They painted the perils of the road in most ghostly colours, and ransacked the pages of history (an unwritten history at present, and existing only in the memories of the oldest inhabitants) for illustrations of the dire results of amateur coaching on the wagon road. All kindly meant, no doubt, but scarcely helpful or to the point. For the point was to get to Cariboo, or rather, Cariboo was the point to get to, and unless we could drive ourselves the point was unattainable."

A bishop speaking to us from the driver's seat of his buckboard as he went on a four hundred mile journey into an unknown country! We could hardly have a more appropriate word from the past than this, nor greater assurance that, with the same clear-sightedness and animated by the same spirit, the Church can accomplish its task in the days that lie ahead.

Godfrey P. Gower

In Loving
Maud Munday
Memory of

Part I

Trumpets in the Mountains, Cymbals by the Sea

And when the builders laid the foundation
of the temple of the Lord,
they set the priests in their apparel with trumpets,
and the Levites the sons of Asaph with cymbals,
to praise the Lord,
after the ordinance of David king of Israel.
And they sang together by course
in praising and giving thanks unto the Lord;
because he is good,
for his mercy endureth forever toward Israel.
And all the people shouted with a great shout,
when they praised the Lord,
because the foundation of the house of the Lord was laid.

– *Ezra*

Queen Victoria's men in British Columbia: Governor James Douglas and Colonel Richard Clement Moody. Paul Goranson's idealized painting shows Royal Engineers and gold miners building the Cariboo Road.

Ned McGowan's War took Moody to Fort Yale. It wasn't much of a war. Governor Douglas thought the charming fugitive from San Francisco vigilantes might lead a rebellion against the new crown colony. So Moody's troop steamed north on the *Enterprise,* Lieutenant Gooch led marines and blue jackets from the *Satellite,* Lieutenant Mayne sailed in a canoe party guided by Myhu-pu-pu, and the Hanging Judge, Matthew Baillie Begbie, went to administer the law. It ended with McGowan pouring them champagne in the Gold Rush camp at Hill's Bar.

Now it was Sunday and men moved in the snow to the courthouse. Colonel Richard Clement Moody of the Royal Engineers was to lead a church service.

"It was the first time in British Columbia that the Liturgy of our Church was read," wrote Moody. "To *me* God in his mercy granted this privilege. The room was crowded full of Hill's Bar men. . .old grey-bearded men, young eager-eyed men, stern middle-aged men of all nations knelt with me before the throne of Grace. . . . Oh! for some of England's Gentlemen, young and ardent as Ministers of God's Words. Let a few such come here and take post against

Colonel Moody went to war, held church instead. "To me God in his mercy granted this privilege."

Fort Yale on the Fraser, 1858. "Gambling houses in full blast," reported *Harper's Weekly*. "The number of houses where liquor is sold is nine of ten." Moody prayed for the miners' souls.

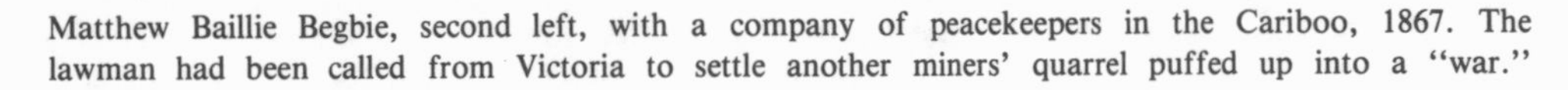

Matthew Baillie Begbie, second left, with a company of peacekeepers in the Cariboo, 1867. The lawman had been called from Victoria to settle another miners' quarrel puffed up into a "war."

The Rev. William Burton Crickmer, first Church of England missionary on the southern mainland.

the enemy of these Miners' souls."

It was January 16, 1859, two months after an eighteen-gun salute from the *Beaver* signaled the raising of the British flag over Fort Langley. Vancouver Island had been a Hudson's Bay Company colony since 1849, governed first by Richard Blanshard, then by James Douglas. In 1858, when the finding of gold on the Thompson and Fraser Rivers began the Fraser Gold Rush, Douglas moved to claim British Columbia for Queen Victoria, and Moody's men were sent from England as Her Majesty's militia.

Hudson's Bay Company missionaries had been west of the Rocky Mountains since 1836. George Simpson, Governor of the Company, had written to London: "I do not know any part of North America where the natives could be civilized and instructed in morality and religion at such a moderate expense and with so much facility as on the Banks of the Columbia River."

In 1856, the Church Missionary Society (CMS) began its work in the fur traders' country, followed the next year by the Society for the Propagation of the Gospel (SPG). On Christmas Day, 1858, the Reverend W. Burton Crickmer of the Colonial Church and School Society landed in Victoria

W.B. Crickmer's sketch of 1859 Derby, showing the missionary preaching from a barrel pulpit. "Very true to life," wrote Vancouver archivist J.S. Matthews. "I know—I have been one of them."

St. John's Church, Derby, envisioned by Crickmer as a many-windowed edifice in the shadow of the mountain named for him. (The 4,500 foot peak between Stave and Alouette Lakes, "lost" for 100 years, was located in 1957 by surveyor Ken Bridge, working from Crickmer's sketch.)

on orders from the Bishop of London. Crickmer went to the Royal Engineers barracks at Derby near Fort Langley and built the Church of St. John the Divine.

In Dickens's London, Dickens's friend, Miss Angela Burdett-Coutts, responded to Colonel Moody's plea for some of England's Gentlemen. Miss Burdett-Coutts, "the richest heiress in London," the woman who refused Prince Louis Napoleon, had endowed the bishoprics of Adelaide and Cape Town. Now she offered the Archbishop of Canterbury £50,000 to establish the Church of England in the Empire's Northwest Pacific colony. The Diocese of British Columbia was created, with two archdeaconries: Vancouver on Vancouver Island and Columbia on the mainland.

On St. Matthias's Day, 1859, in Westminster Abbey, the Reverend George Hills, Vicar of Great Yarmouth and Canon of Norwich, was consecrated first Lord Bishop of British Columbia. Mr. Hills demurred that another with superior qualifications might be found, but he was Miss Burdett-Coutts's choice. He preached a farewell sermon at

Crickmer's church as it really was--and remained, a century later, then at Maple Ridge. The church was floated across the river to its new parish after Crickmer moved to Yale.

Pre-Raphaelite sketch of George Hills, first Lord Bishop of British Columbia, probably circa 1859.

The first Holy Trinity Church, New Westminster. John Sheepshanks and settlers cleared the land, a Royal Engineers architect designed the building. Rectory (with ladder) at front.

St. James's, Piccadilly: "Brethren, pray for us."

In England, Bishop Hills recruited priests for the new diocese. Two of them arrived in British Columbia before he did. One was the Reverend R.J. Dundas, who took a prefabricated iron church to Victoria. The other was a towering, red-bearded Cambridge graduate, the Reverend John Sheepshanks, who traveled up the Fraser River to New Westminster, Moody's choice as the colony's capital.

"I looked up a long stretch of the river," remembered Sheepshanks, "and there I saw a bit of a clearing in the dense forest. Mighty trees were lying about in confusion, as though a giant with one sweep of his arm had mown them down. . . .And between the prostrate trees and stumps there were a few huts, one small collection of wooden stores, some sheds and tents, giving signs of a population of about 250 people."

The 250, most of them men, were English, French, German, Portuguese, African, Chinese, Mexican, American and Indian, a mixture of nationalities in which Bishop Hills would discern "a foreshadowing of the gathering in of all nations to the fold of Christ." But if they were like the gold miners SPG missionary James Gammage worked among between Hope and Quesnel, they were "very keen for gain" and some even might have lacked "every moral quality that ennobles or dignifies humanity."

Sheepshanks moved his six-feet-three frame into a seven-by-ten log cabin, stuffed the cracks with moss and hung a calico curtain over a hole in the wall. (A neighbor used gin bottles for windows.) "I really am quite well off," wrote Sheepshanks in his diary.

He held his first church service in the customs house, sounding a Chinese gong to summon the faithful. Seven men came. "A spiritual desert," muttered Sheepshanks.

Services were being held in the army camp schoolhouse by the Reverend H.P. Wright, chaplain to the Royal Engineers, but it was evident that the capital city (especially a *Royal* City, named by Queen Victoria) required a church that was a church, not a schoolhouse or a customs house; so Sheepshanks pried £1,000 out of friends in England, led a land-clearing bee, and laid the foundations for Holy Trinity Church.

Captain A.R. Lempriere of the Royal Engineers designed the building, the cornerstone was laid by Governor Douglas, and the church was consecrated on Advent Sunday, 1860, by Bishop Hills. Each Sunday, Colonel

The Rev. John Sheepshanks, re-creating his Fraser River experiences for a London photographer.

Crickmer drew his wife ("head nurse") and himself ("under nurse") with son William in 1859. Crickmer advised his boys to try "facetious skits and caricatures—pungent and to the point."

Moody's red-coated company marched to church, led by a band. "The singing was good," said a satisfied Sheepshanks. Pews were offered for rent: $5.00 for the first four, $4.00 for the middle four, $3.00 for four in the back. The last two pews were for strangers.

That same year, Sheepshanks rode with Bishop Hills up the Fraser Canyon to Lillooet on missions to the Thompson River Indians. "I addressed them," said the Bishop, "told them who I was, why I had come, showed them the Bible, told them it was the word of God, we knew what it contained, they did not."

Sheepshanks described the caravan: "First came the tall, grave, dignified Bishop. So tall was he, and so long of limb, that riding on a big horse, if he dropped his whip to the ground, he could pick it up while still in the saddle."

The young minister liked to ride along, hands in pockets, whistling. One day, Bishop Hills said, "I cannot think how you can indulge in that habit of whistling. It is so undignified. I might say so – unclerical!" Sheepshanks dutifully unpuckered. But after a while, he would find himself "half a mile behind the others, and lo! again the sombre forest would re-echo with the popular airs of the period."

Sheepshanks learned Chinook so he could teach the Indians prayers; went spearfishing for salmon; taught some Chinese men to read English. In 1862, when the Fraser River was frozen for four months, he played hockey. "Business is at a standstill," he wrote cheerfully. "Sleigh-driving and hockey have been the order of the day." In his diary, he noted, "all the bed-clothes. . .are stiff with ice. The bread is frozen. . .the ink is solid. . .the camphine will not burn. I like the weather."

New Westminster's Gold Rush boom was over by 1864 and bankruptcy was spreading through the colony. Sheepshanks went back to England, collection plate in hand. While he was there, Holy Trinity Church burned down (the parishioners looked accusingly at the heavy-smoking sexton) and the rector was required to pass the plate around again. He came back with sufficient funds to bring sandstone from Salt Spring Island for "the first stone church on the Pacific Coast."

Sheepshanks left New Westminster forever in 1866, returning to England in Phileas Fogg fashion: across the Pacific, into the Sandwich Islands, over Northern China and

Bishop Hills, ready to ride north with the word of God to the Thompson River Indians.

The precipitous China Bar Bluff on the Fraser Canyon road travelled by miners and missionaries.

Sheepshanks in his travelling garb. "Whistling," said the bishop, "was so unclerical!"

Mongolia, across the Gobi Desert, through Siberia and the Ural Mountains to Moscow. He travelled most of it alone, unarmed and on foot. Whistling. In England, he became Vicar of Bolton in Yorkshire, married Miss Margaret Ryott, and fathered thirteen children.

John Sheepshanks preached his last sermon in British Columbia at Christ Church Cathedral, Victoria. "While I was preaching," he recalled, "I observed the brown face, black hair and impassive countenance of an Indian in the congregation, listening with stolid attention. When the service was over, I lingered a while, saying goodbye to the officials, so that when the Bishop and clergy had departed I was left behind. In the porch, I found the Indian waiting for me.

"'How are you, Chief?' he said. 'My heart is with you.'

"'You know me?' I asked.

"'Oh, yes, Chief. I have been at New Westminster and up Fraser River and have heard of you.'

"'And what is your name?' I asked.

"'I am Paul Legaic.'

"'You are *Legaic*?'

"'I was Legaic. Now I am *Paul* Legaic.'"

Legaic, the Tsimshian leader, "the ruthless, cruel chief, the great medicine man, the cannibal, the murderer." William Duncan of the Church Missionary Society had converted and baptized him, giving him the Christian name Paul. "And here he was," marveled Sheepshanks, "with the evil spirits cast out of him, 'clothed and in his right mind,' a signal and convincing instance of Divine grace. One could not but recognize the power of the Gospel, and adore the Divine mercy."

Before getting on board the ship for the South Pacific, Sheepshanks gave Bishop Hills papers for a piece of land he had bought near Burrard Inlet. The bishop was to continue making the miniscule yearly payments. But he didn't. The land became the centre of Vancouver.

1879. The Zulus were defeated at Ulundi. St. Enoch's Station in Glasgow was lit by electricity. Dostoyevsky wrote *The Brothers Karamazov;* James, *Daisy Miller;* Ibsen, *A Doll's House.* The first electric tram was driven at the Berlin Trade Exhibition. Cezanne, Manet, Renoir and Degas were painting in Paris. James Ritty invented the cash register. And in the *McCabe and Mrs. Miller* milieu of British Columbia, Bishop Hills decided it was time for two new dioceses and two new bishops.

George Hills had looked saintly and poetic in a Pre-Raphaelite sketch. Now he was tough and leathery, like a surpliced John A. MacDonald. He had had his battle with the evangelical Dean Cridge in Victoria and there was Duncan at Metlakatla with the same disagreeable views. Striding along Fort Street with Judge Begbie, the bishop made plans for the division of the 390,344 square mile diocese into three.

At the 1878 Synod, he told delegates, "Cariboo, Kamloops, Nicola, Chilliwack, the Lower Fraser Valley and Cassiar are needing the ministrations of the Church, but we send them no supply. . . .could faithful ministers of God be sent, the blessing as elsewhere would follow, and great good be done. . . ."

Bishop Hills, 1890—a surpliced Sir John A. MacDonald, ruler of a 390,344 square mile diocese.

Charles Woods of Trinity College, Dublin, first Archdeacon of Columbia (now Vancouver) 1860-95.

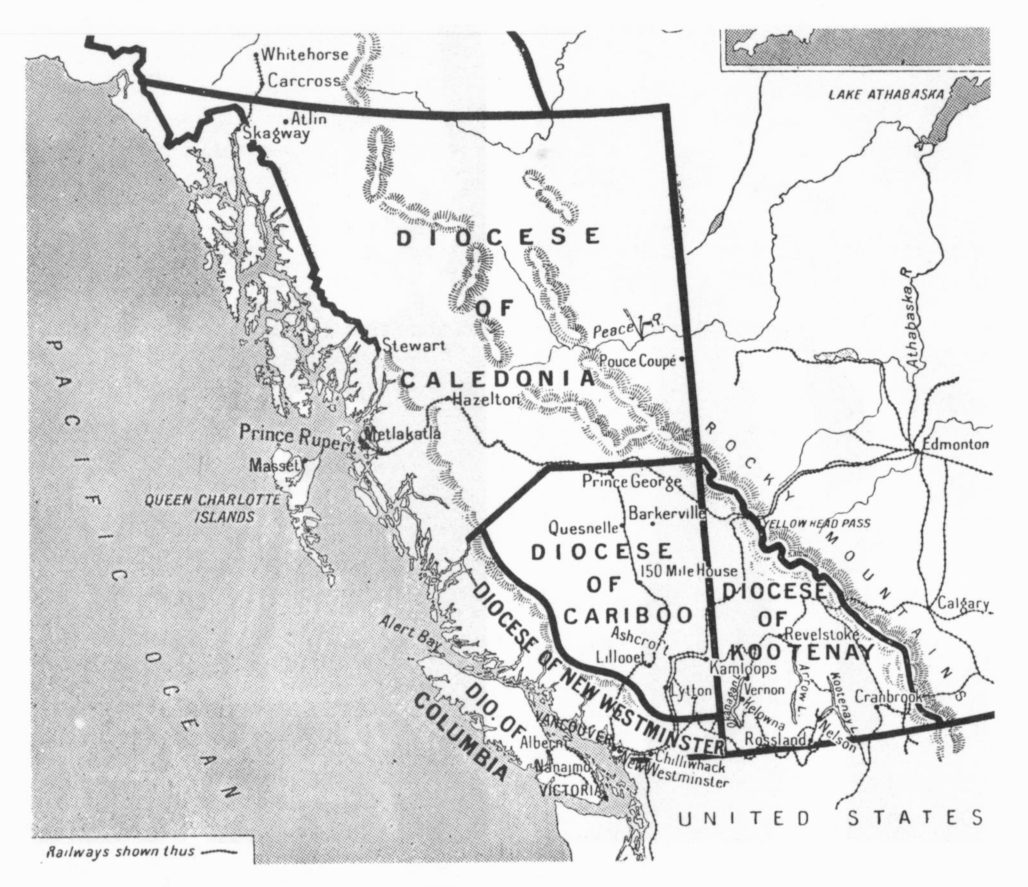

British Columbia carved into new dioceses. Kootenay remained under New Westminster until 1915, Cariboo until 1925. The map is from the mission magazine *Across the Rockies*.

The synod then approved this resolution: "That this synod is of the opinion that a division of the diocese into three separate dioceses, viz. (1) Vancouver Island, (2) New Westminster, (3) Caledonia, with a view to forming a provincial organization for British Columbia, is very desirable, and that this synod cordially supports the endeavour of the Lord Bishop to carry out the scheme when in England,"

In England, Bishop Hills "laid the resolution before the Archbishop of Canterbury." Hills had made a similar proposal sixteen years earlier; but this time he received the Archbishop's "cordial support; and after many months of hard work in raising endowment funds, I had the happiness of a successful result."

Vancouver Island would remain as the Diocese of British Columbia; Northern British Columbia would become the Diocese of Caledonia; the rest of the territory, 400 miles long and 400 miles wide, from Burrard Inlet south to the U.S. border, north to Nechako and east to Fort Steele, including the Cariboo, the Kootenays and the Fraser, Thompson and Upper Columbia Valleys, would become the Diocese of New Westminster.

Acton Windeyer Sillitoe was then chaplain to the British Legation at Darmstadt, the capital of the German Republic of Hesse. In 1876, he had been appointed British chaplain at Geneva. The next year he went to Germany to serve, among others, Princess Alice, Grand Duchess of Hesse-Darmstadt, daughter of Queen Victoria, mother of the future Czarina Alexandra.

The Grand Duchess had been unsettled by the theories of the renegade theologian David Friedrich Strauss (as her daughter was to be swayed by Rasputin). Strauss's 1835 *Life of Jesus* attempted to show myth at the root of the gospel narratives. He preached scientific materialism and rejected the concept of immortality. By 1872, when he published *The Old and the New Faith,* he was entirely hostile to Christianity.

Sillitoe's work at Darmstadt "was signalized by his great influence over the Princess Alice and her children, especially her daughters. . .he was undoubtedly the means, under God, of bringing the Princess back from Strauss and unbelief to the happiness of the Faith."

At least, so wrote "one high in influence in the Church of England," reported Sillitoe's biographer, Herbert H. Gowen. In the Lambeth Palace Library, there are other opinions of Sillitoe's work.

"There is a portion of the English community very Evangelical," wrote one critic, "and I must say Mr. Sillitoe did not display much wisdom or discretion in dealing with them. There were others, like the Grand Duchess herself, who had come under the influence of Strauss in times past, but were fighting their way through difficulties and doubts to a clear, strong faith in God and Christ. With such Mr. Sillitoe had. . .little sympathy, and of the nature of their daily struggle he had little appreciation. He could not understand how they should want a kind of help which he himself had never needed."

Acton Sillitoe was 39 years old, and perhaps he still spoke with a New South Wales accent ("Let us pr'y"), for he had been born in Sydney and lived there until he was 14.

He was, his wife wrote later, "never very strong" and, when he was a child, bathing in the sea was prescribed for him. The Sillitoe family lived by the Bay of Sydney, and Sillitoe père would take his son to the beach.

Acton Windeyer Sillitoe—from the courts of Europe to the wild frontier of New Westminster.

Acton and Violet Sillitoe, a Regent Street portrait taken before they boarded the *Sarmatian*.

But the small boy disliked the chill of the waves, so his father good-naturedly (and imaginatively) carried with them each morning a pitcher of hot water. Down they went to the sea, the father holding Acton by one hand, the pitcher in the other. There he would pour the hot water into the ocean, and Acton would uncomplainingly follow, convinced that the water had been made tolerably warm.

The Sillitoes went to England in 1854. Acton attended King's College School, London, and Pembroke College, Cambridge. He was ordained to the priesthood in 1870 by Bishop Selwyn of Lichfield (who had been a missionary bishop in New Zealand and Melanesia).

Sillitoe served in the parishes of Brierley Hill, Staffordshire; All Saints', Wolverhampton; and Ellenbrook. "I cannot tell you much about Mr. Sillitoe," went another of those confidential communications to the Archbishop of Canterbury. "He was not long in this diocese. . .he was long enough, however, to upset things rather. . . . If I remember right, it was not a very grave offence, nothing worse than the introduction of *Hymns Ancient & Modern,* but I thought it showed want of discretion."

But the name Acton Windeyer Sillitoe had been put forward by the Society for the Propagation of the Gospel and it was the SPG which was to sponsor the work of the new diocese. (The CMS took Caledonia.) "Bishop Hills asked me if I could suggest a good man," wrote "one high in influence," "and I at once recommended Mr. Sillitoe." (It has been suggested that Sillitoe was recommended to the Archbishop by one incomparably high in influence: the Queen-Empress herself, in which case no amount of carping about *Hymns Ancient & Modern* was going to keep Sillitoe from getting his amethyst ring.)

"It may be," huffed the Sillitoe non-enthusiast, "that in a larger sphere, and with a sense of a wider responsibility such as the position of a bishop might be expected to bring, Mr. Sillitoe will display a more extended sympathy and a greater tact. [But] goodness and sincerity without wisdom and tact may not enable one to deal successfully with the varied circumstances which surround the young and energetic life of our Church in the Colonies."

Sillitoe had a few doubts of his own. One of those who had urged his selection said, "I well recollect his coming to me and saying he wished I had let him alone, that he was by no means the man I took him to be, that he was very human. . . ."

The first Bishop of New Westminster was consecrated on All Saints' Day, 1879, in the Croydon parish church of St. John, Baptist. Archbishop Tait of Canterbury performed the consecration, assisted by a quintet of bishops, among them George Hills. Six months later, Bishop Sillitoe and his 24-year-old wife, Violet, sailed for Canada. The Sillitoes' last church service in England was a celebration of Holy Communion at St. Margaret's, Anfield. The rector probably had a word of advice for them: he was the Reverend John Sheepshanks.

The Sillitoes sailed aboard the *Sarmatian* from Liverpool, travelling through "a hundred and forty miles of ice." The new bishop conducted services on board. In the months before leaving England, he had organized a home committee, addressed missionary societies and tried to engage interest in the frontier diocese. His first episcopal letter to New Westminster was dated November 13, 1879:

Yale, 1883—headquarters for Canadian Pacific Railway builders. Indians, prospectors, gandy dancers gathered in front of the Hudson's Bay store. It was a long way from Hesse-Darmstadt.

Charles Baskett, Missionary at Hastings. His parish stretched from the Fraser to Prince Rupert.

"I enter on my holy office in the full conviction that He Who hath called me will be with me to further my weak endeavours, and to supply all my defects. . . . I have had a letter from Archdeacon Wright and a copy of a report on the spiritual destitution of the mainland. The letter is a gloomy one, but it has not made me gloomy. Let us take courage and go forward."

In another letter, Bishop Sillitoe wrote: "I hope to be in a most real sense a 'father' to my clergy, and though they may differ as widely as the wide comprehensiveness of our Church permits, I shall never as *Bishop* lean more to one way of thinking than another. I shall claim the right to hold my own views and to express them, and to place them in the most favourable light I can, but I shall never regard a fellow-worker with less affection because he fails to see things from my standpoint; and my clergy will, I hope, honour my fairness in this respect by equal confidence in one another."

About the time the Sillitoes were walking up the wharf at New Westminster, going to Holy Trinity Church to sing the *Te Deum,* a former resident of the city was writing to the *Times* of India: "Sir: New Westminster is no place for European gentlemen. It is a dense forest full of panthers, bears, wolves, deer and grouse. But besides the shooting of these, there is nothing else to do. The life of a miner is a round of swearing, drinking and gambling. The most bare-faced immorality goes on publicly and knows no shame."

Acton Sillitoe's first letter home said, "This is really a very lovely place. . . ."

New Westminster had 2,600 people and 20 saloons. Besides the new bishop, the entire diocesan staff was three priests and one deacon. Would-be clergy lodged with SPG missionary Charles Baskett, in a house built of bunched-together sappers' shacks. (One tyro priest slept under a funeral pall.)

Bishop Sillitoe organized a committee of the SPG, held a congregational meeting in the Drill Shed, rode the stage to saw mills at Moodyville and Burrard Inlet, took the steamer to logging camps on the North Arm. Men in the camps liked his "frank and manly spirit."

With Baskett, he travelled down river to the salmon canneries at Ladner's Landing and told the people who came to hear him that if they raised £80, he'd match it, and find them a parson. Thomas Ladner, a prospector from California who had stopped at Robert's Point (now Delta) and was a partner

in the Delta Cannery, began the building of All Saints' Church. (As magistrate, Ladner also facilitated the tiling of the church roof by sentencing a Welsh slater charged with drunkenness to do the job.) All Saints' became the first church built in the new diocese. It stands today, framed with poplars, by Chilukthan Slough.

The bishop travelled to Yale, still a tough, rowdy town at the southern end of the Cariboo Trail. "Live Missionary at Yale" was the newspaper headline. (In fact, there had been a live missionary there for fourteen years: the SPG's John Booth Good. On Vancouver Island in the early 1860s, Good had gone from house to house, vaccinating Indians against smallpox. In 1866 he responded to a Chinook message: *"Lytton siwashes tum tum mikacloosh hyaek chaco."* —"The Lytton Indians think you had better make haste and come." In 1867, the onetime Lincolnshire schoolmaster opened the Indian Boys' School at Lytton.)

At Yale, Sillitoe appointed Silas Nalee catechist, trained a choir, married an Indian girl to a Chinese rancher, helped fight a fire, buried two men killed in the blaze, and held services for gandy dancers and Indians at a Canadian Pacific Railway camp. "The air was heavy with the scent of meadowsweet

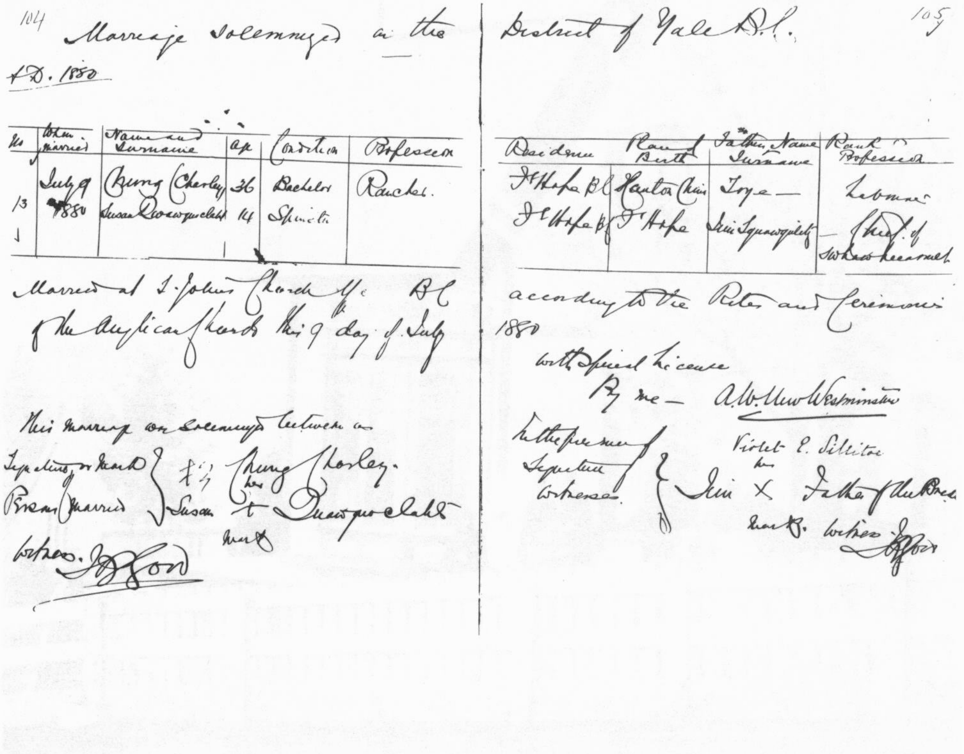
104 Marriage solemnized in the District of Yale B.C. 105

A.D. 1880

No	When married	Name and Surname	Age	Condition	Profession	Residence	Rank Birth	Father's Name Surname	Rank Profession
13	July 9 1880	Chung Charley	36	Bachelor	Rancher	Ft Hope BC	Canton China	Toye	Labourer
		Susan Quawquoclaht	14	Spinster		Ft Hope BC	Ft Hope	Jim Squawquoclaht	Chief of [illegible]

Married at St. John's Church Yale BC according to the Rites and Ceremonies of the Anglican Church this 9 day of July 1880 with special licence

By me — A.W. New Westminster

This marriage was solemnized between us: Chung Charley, Susan Quawquoclaht [illegible]

In the presence of: Violet E. Sillitoe; Jim [his X mark], Father of the Bride

Witness: J.B. Good

Bishop Sillitoe's record book, noting the 1880 marriage in Yale of Chung Charlie and Susan Quawquoclaht. The 14-year-old bride was formally designated "spinster." The handwriting is Sillitoe's.

St. Mary's Mount ("Hotel Sillitoe") welcomed prime ministers, governors general, clergy retreatants. "An English tone pervaded the little society," wrote Bishop Sillitoe in 1880 Sapperton.

and syringa," reported a newspaperman. "The Bishop preached, and one gentleman interpreted to the Yale Indians, while another translated for the edification of the Spuzzum Indians."

The Sillitoes lived in the Archdeaconry House in Sapperton, which they renamed St. Mary's Mount. On the grounds was the church of St. Mary the Virgin, built in 1865 by former members of the Royal Engineers. (Moody's force of surveyors and architects, carpenters and masons, et al, had disbanded in 1863.) It was, wrote the bishop, "a model of what all wooden churches might be.... It was the 'fashionable church'...Government House stood near; officials and their staff had their residences round about; an English tone pervaded the little society."

The house became known as "Hotel Sillitoe," and in it they entertained the Marquis of Lorne and Princess Louise (Princess Alice's sister), Lord Lansdowne, Lord Stanley and Sir John A. MacDonald. The Princess made sketches, sang duets with Violet (she alto, Violet soprano) and went for a ride in the bishop's buckboard. "There was a great gathering of Indians," wrote Violet, "to see the Queen's Papoose."

Violet Sillitoe was then, she tells us, "very young and very shy", although in a photograph of that period she appears remarkably self-controlled, a slight, rather severe woman with a pince nez, curled hair worn high. The bishop was a handsome man with Edwardian beard and moustaches and an open, uncomplicated gaze.

The other residents of St. Mary's Mount included George, an Indian servant; Gin and Sing, two Chinese servants; various canine companions – Sam and Bran first, Piper, Grip and Jingo later; and Punch, a handsome racehorse, a birthday present from Acton to Violet. The specialty of the house was salmon, then being sold to the canneries by the Indians for one halfpenny a fish, and provided without charge to the bishop's household. *"Toujours saumon,"* sighed the bishop.

In the autumn of 1880, the Sillitoes began the first of their Pauline travels throughout the immense diocese. With George and Punch, they took a steamer to Hope. There they hired two guides, Antoine and Susap, and rented six horses. They rode off into the Okanagan, the bishop baptizing along the way. The party slept on cedar beds in groves of fir trees, by trout streams, in forests full of grouse and in one – burned, bleached – full of caterpillars. They pushed through a marsh, their horses knee-high in

The Marquis of Lorne, Governor General of Canada, visited B.C.—and the Sillitoes—in 1882.

New Westminster scene drawn by Lord Lorne. Princess Louise also sketched while at Hotel Sillitoe.

The first St. James's Church in 1886, the year Vancouver was incorporated as a city. Spratt's Oilery and the government reserve land which became Stanley Park are in the background. The little girl stands near the site of the corner of Main and Alexander Streets in Gastown.

mud. They bathed in creeks. The bishop preached at a service in Mr. Forbes Vernon's Mission Valley barn, at which hens and chipmunks gave their testimony. They speared salmon at an Indian fishing camp and visited two gentlemen at Ashcroft who kept foxhounds to hunt coyotes. One moonlit night, lying in their tent, they heard a thundering sound and looked out to see a pack of wild horses gallop past. In six weeks, they journeyed 800 miles.

Back in New Westminster, Bishop Sillitoe worked on diocesan organization, wrote reports for the SPG, held night school classes at St. Mary's Mount, saw to the building of schools, preached to the prisoners at the Provincial Penitentiary, urged temperance, and rowed up and down the Fraser to take services at logging camps – services to which, sometimes, no one but the bishop came.

The diocese's first service of confirmation was held June 27, 1880. Thirty-five candidates were presented for the laying on of hands. The first ordination was November 14, when Charles Blanchard was made a deacon. March 13, 1881, George Ditcham was priested.

In the forest between the sawmill settlements of Granville and Hastings Mill, land had been chosen for a church, to be called St. James's. The church was built, and Bishop Sillitoe dedicated it May 14, 1881. The first priests in the community, Charles Baskett and George Ditcham, served a parish stretching from the Fraser River to what is now Prince Rupert.

"Oh, dear young brethren," the bishop told his men, in Sapperton on retreats, "remember that wherever your Lord sends you, He goes with you. He does not bid you go in your own strength, but in His. Your weakness in Him is omnipotent power; your foolishness in Him omniscient wisdom. 'You can of your own selves do nothing, but you can do all things through Christ strengthening you.' You can 'bind up the broken-hearted' by His love working in you; you can 'preach deliverance to the captives' by His Spirit operating through you; by the light of His word you shall recover sight to the blind, and by the authority of His commission you shall heal those whom sin hath bruised. 'God was in Christ reconciling the world unto Himself,' and Christ in you will carry on the work."

A railway handcar crossing a chasm—a way for the Sillitoes to make their parish visits.

The clergy of the diocese at synod in the 1880s. Standing, from left: George Ditcham, E.L. Wright, Archdeacon Woods, Henry Fiennes-Clinton, Charles Croucher, (unidentified clergyman), Richard Small, (unidentified clergyman). Seated are Bishop Sillitoe and Henry Edwardes.

On October 3, 1882, Bishop Sillitoe presided at the first Diocesan Synod. The diocese then included the territory that now makes up three dioceses: New Westminster, Kootenay and Cariboo. And Acton and Violet continued to travel the territory.

"We travelled in all sorts of ways," wrote Violet. "Riding, driving, canoeing, walking, working ourselves along the railway on a handcar. . . ."

"A handcar on a single line of railway, where freight trains run independently of time-tables, and where curves are as sharp as they have to be in this gorge of the Fraser River, is an exciting kind of travelling," wrote Acton. "In many places the track overhangs the river at a height of several hundred feet; at others it is carried over deep gullies or ravines on wooden trestles. . . .The platform of a handcar. . . is a position from which one can appreciate without effort the 'chances of this mortal life.'"

Once the couple crossed the Fraser Canyon in a basket, Archdeacon Woods's daughter squeezed in with them. Once, when Acton was stretched out in the buckboard with a nest of boils on his back, Violet drove the team. And sometimes, to get where they were going, they fought their way through fire.

"Worst," said Violet, "were the forest fires. . .the big trees crackling and burning on either side, falling every now and again with a crash, the air dense with smoke and the flames from the burning underbrush driven by the wind. . . ."

"During the day," she wrote of one journey, "we had to drive through several fires. . . .The boss told the Bishop to whip the ponies 'all he knew how,' and gallop through. . .the large cedar falling directly after. . . .Hardly had we driven a mile before we found a tree fallen right across the road, with no possibility of getting round it, so we unhitched, and the Bishop chopped out the smaller branches. He then made the ponies jump over, and we proceeded to lift over the buckboard."

"The point was to get to Cariboo," said the bishop, "or rather, Cariboo was the point to get to."

The bishop organized the New Westminster Choral Union and conducted them in concert. Violet sang. Each year's program schedule included Handel's *The Messiah.* On their travels, Acton carried a baritone concertina, an organ-toned accordion, which

Preachers travelled on horseback—what Father Pat called "the hurricane deck of a cayuse."

Stagecoach at Barkerville, ready to leave for Quesnel. Travelling in the territory, the Sillitoes held church services wherever they could draw a crowd—barrooms, general stores, railway stations, roadside camps. Acton and Violet drove their own buckboard and groomed their own horses.

he played wherever church services could be arranged: barrooms, general stores, roadside camps, railway stations. And he was always delighted to improvise entertainments, in such settings as Barkerville's Theatre Royal.

"A visit to Barkerville was never complete without a concert," wrote Violet, "and I had to take the part of the *prima donna.* After the very generous applause that greeted the conclusion of my first song, I was surprised to hear something fall on the stage close to me, and, on looking down, saw a 50¢ piece. Others followed, with an occasional silver dollar. . . ."

When J.B. Good left the Indian Mission in 1882, Bishop Sillitoe brought from England the Reverend Richard Small. Small eventually became superintendent of Indian missions in the diocese and was made Archdeacon of Yale. He was, wrote church historian Frank Peake, "the apostle to the Thompson River Indians." His assistants included a minister named E.L. Wright (called "Down" Wright to distinguish him from another minister named Wright and stationed in the Kootenays. He, naturally, was "Up" Wright.)

Barkerville—Billy Barker's Cariboo boom town—for a time, the most exciting place north of San Francisco. St. Saviour's, the church of gold miners and saloon girls, still holds services.

Prospectors at Ne'er Do Well Mine near Barkerville panning for gold at Grouse Creek. Later, they could go to the Theatre Royal and hear Violet sing and Acton play accordion.

There was intense competition among missionaries of various denominations for the presumed truant souls of the Indians. "Down" Wright was pleased to be able to report: "I have just heard of an Indian woman, who was supposed to have died and has come to life again just as she was being put into a coffin. When she came to, she said she had been to a place where some people were miserable and some happy, and all the happy ones belonged to the Church of England! This has had a great effect upon the unbaptized Indians, who now say they are all coming to us."

"I used sometimes to think," wrote Violet Sillitoe, "that the Indians were nearer to [the Bishop's] heart than any other members of his flock."

"One summer," she remembered, "we spent some weeks camping out near the different Indian villages, and in the evening, the Indians would gather round the Bishop for instruction, and this would go on until past midnight, for whenever the Bishop would wish to stop, the Indians would urge him to continue, and how he loved this work. . . ."

The bishop was consulted by the chiefs on social as well as religious matters. "The

Bishop Sillitoe and some of the thousand Indians who gathered near Lytton for Whitsunday, 1884. "A glorious day," wrote Sillitoe, "in the secluded valley of Pootanie. There was no sound from heaven, no cloven tongues of fire, but there was the felt presence of God the Holy Ghost."

All Hallows' School, Yale, established in 1888 for "the cultivation of womanly virtues." Conducted by Sisters Elizabeth, Amy and Alice of the Community of All Hallows', Ditchingham, Norfolk, it continued its work until after World War I, then merged with St. George's School, Lytton.

whole throng of men, women and children gathered on the slope in front of my tent," he wrote. "I had the happiness of restoring harmony to two wigwams."

Violet Sillitoe remembered "Indians wandering up the hill – the Chiefs first, then the other men on horseback. . .then . . .the women and children. We had to shake hands with every one, even the tiniest newborn infant, the mother holding out its hand for us to take. . . .We shook hands with nearly a thousand."

One of the Indians wrote, "We built a rough church and altar, the clergy and Indians all working together. The church was built of green brush and flowers, and we hung up all our flags."

"Services went on all day," wrote Violet, with "the baptism of 19 babies, the Bishop standing by the side of the creek and using the water which flowed at his feet."

Bishop Sillitoe enjoyed a potlatch ("A *potlatch,"* Violet explained in a letter, "is a large party to which the giver invites all his *tillicums* (friends) and gives away his presents"); but he thought the medicine man an "evil influence." To replace this powerful figure, he brought to the diocese a medical missionary, Dr. Arthur Pearse, and built St. Bartholomew's Indian Hospital at Lytton and another hospital at Shulus.

A day school was opened in Yale (some of the funds were provided by Indians of Yankee Flat who had been working on CPR construction crews), and Sister Elizabeth, Sister Amy and Sister Alice came from the Community of All Hallows in Ditchingham, Norfolk, to conduct a school for Indian girls.

The coming of the missionaries had changed the lives of the Indians – some of them, at least. "Men whose histories were written in blood and sorceries," wrote Bishop Hills, "had become humble and teachable disciples of the Lord Jesus." And, reported the SPG, "the Indian converts, by their consistent Christian lives, were frequently a rebuke to the Europeans."

But Indian lives were also changed, said Bishop Sillitoe, by "the usual effects of approximation to the white man – drunkenness and fornication." He lamented "the crooked ways by which bad intoxicating liquors find their ways into the hands of Indians [causing] untold misery to the Indians who wish to live quiet and orderly." Richard Small and Henry Edwardes, priest at the Lytton Indian Mission, described the Indians as "once simple, happy, healthy, free. . .the victims of our sins, our vices, and diseases."

Sillitoe called government work among the Indians a "policy of promises. . .as unsafe as it is unjust. . .as cruel as it is short-sighted." He told the Royal Colonial Institute, "they [the Indians] give the Government so little trouble that the Government feel under no necessity to give themselves any trouble on their behalf. A number of officials are employed to look after them whose duties are certainly the reverse of arduous. The title of 'Old Tomorrow,' applied by the Indians themselves to a very prominent Canadian statesman, sums up epigrammatically the character of Indian administration in British Columbia." He concluded, "between the Dominion Government and the Provincial Government the Indian administration has got into such a muddle that nothing can be done. . . ."

As for the church, a diocese with thirteen priests serving 160,000 square miles in the mid-1880s had not enough men to minister to all the tribes that wanted them. After one journey, Sillitoe wrote, "The chief. . .said neither himself nor his people could think what the Church was doing to leave him thus

"Sunday after Payday"—an 1884 artist's picture of Yale, a tough, rowdy Gold Rush town. Missionary James Gammage found men "keen for gain" and lacking "every moral quality." The Church of St. John the Divine watches over the raucous scene—a fine frontier tableau.

entirely alone and neglected. . . .All he said was in sorrow, not in anger. I replied with the oft-repeated excuse of 'no men' – God only knows how my soul revolts against it." On his return trip, "I had to listen to the same bitter complaints repeated, and to reply in the same strain. . . . One cannot help feeling that the Church will have to answer for many lost souls during these past years of trouble and grievous temptation to the Indian tribes."

Money problems began early, both for the diocese and the bishop. The bishop's income was less than $3,000 a year, and in 1882, after spending $4,253 of his own funds on church work, his bank account was overdrawn by $3,234. In the colony, wrote Holy Trinity memoirist Leslie T.H. Pearson, "times were hard and work scarce, owing to a trade depression in both lumbering and fishing."

"I try hard not to think of money," wrote Bishop Sillitoe, "but the thought will creep in sometimes. . . .the responsibility of seeing people paid is very heavy." In 1884, he wrote to London, "The simple fact. . .is that the diocese at this moment is insolvent."

In 1885, he wrote again: "Two churches are now closed, and a third will be closed at the end of a month; two have been reduced to fortnightly services. One school was closed last June, and another is to be closed at Christmas. We are in debt to the clergy for stipends, due on June 30th last, about £90, and we have about £20 in hand to meet this and the stipends falling due on the 30th inst.; and I have had to borrow money on the mortgage of Church property to meet liabilities which could not wait, and have made advances myself to the very utmost of my ability. 'Why not come home and beg yourself?' say some people. I cannot afford to come home at present, but further, it ought not to be necessary. . . where is the use of great missionary societies like SPG and CMS, or of the multitude of lesser 'committees,' 'councils,' and 'agencies,' if, after all, the Bishops have to do the begging? We are *sent by the Church* to do her work . . .it is a degradation of our office to have to make 'appeals' to conjure pence out of people's pockets." Nevertheless, he went home – twice – to beg himself.

The growing country made growing demands upon the church. A.W. Vowell wrote from the Kootenays: "Right Rev. and Dear Sir: I am induced to trouble you. . . hoping you may have it in your power to meet the views of people residing here, both as affects educational and religious matters. It has been decided by the CPR that Donald is to be the most important station this side of Winnipeg. Large machine shops and round houses are to be maintained, and some three hundred and fifty or four hundred men will be kept here by the CPR. Many of these fill important positions, and members of all classes coming in have families, but the superintendent tells me they object to this place as being unfit. . .there being no schools, no churches. . . ."

St. Peter's, the first church in the Rocky Mountains, was built, and in 1887, Bishop Sillitoe – back from England, the Lambeth Conference and Queen Victoria's Jubilee Service – celebrated Holy Communion at Donald.

The priest posted to the parish was the Reverend Henry Irwin, the legendary Father Pat of the Kootenays, an Irishman born in the shadow of the Wicklow Mountains and schooled at Keble College. At Oxford, he rowed in the Torpids and the Eights, played in the College Eleven and the Varsity Fifteen, and was a champion boxer. He had been a new curate at Rugby when he began corresponding with Bishop Sillitoe; in 1885, he found himself in Kamloops, a parson on

Railwaymen in the Kootenays, where Father Pat (Henry Irwin) won a name for derring-do.

horseback to miners, railroad builders and settlers south from the Nicola Valley to the United States and east from Ashcroft to the Rockies. "Thanks for the. . .riding pants you sent me," he wrote his friends at Rugby, "but after about 300 miles, they went to pieces, and I had to get into a vile kind of garment they call 'overalls,' striped like a zebra and cut like a sailor's pantaloons."

From Donald, high in the mountains, he travelled down the Arrow Lakes to the mining camp at Nelson on "the hurricane deck of a cayuse" and to Wild Horse Creek near the Tobacco Plains after hearing that "mountain fever was raging among the North West Mounted Police."

J.G. Thynne remembered that Andrew Onderdonk, who supervised construction of the Canadian Pacific Railway through the Fraser Canyon, "always told Father Pat to use a speeder or a handcar whenever he wanted to go anywhere on the line. One day coming from Eagle Pass to Kamloops, Father Pat rode on a large, four-man handcar. They stopped. . .to pick up the Section Boss. Father Pat had his coat off and was helping to pump the car. The Boss said, 'What the hell are you doing there? Get off!' He grabs Father Pat, Pat swung an uppercut on him. Pat went to Kamloops on the car; the Boss laid where Pat put him."

That winter, high in the Selkirks, Father Pat led what he called "the strangest funeral procession that ever passed on earth."

"An avalanche came thundering down Mount Carrol," he wrote, "and came right across the valley and struck the track, turned right up grade and smashed into two engines and the snowplough, burying them completely, and 16 men with them."

One of the buried railroaders had been the husband of a friend of Father Pat, and when the woman became "wild with anxiety," the priest led a party of men, on snowshoes and toboggan, to bring back the body.

"We had to climb over slides between the snowslides. . .trailing across the hills with a coffin swinging on a pole. . .listening for the avalanche. . .like artillery booming away. . . the slide rushing into the gulch at 100 miles a minute."

"I think of all queer frisks," wrote Father Pat, "this day's was the greatest I ever had. Of course, I should not have done it unless the poor wife was here fretting her heart away. . . "

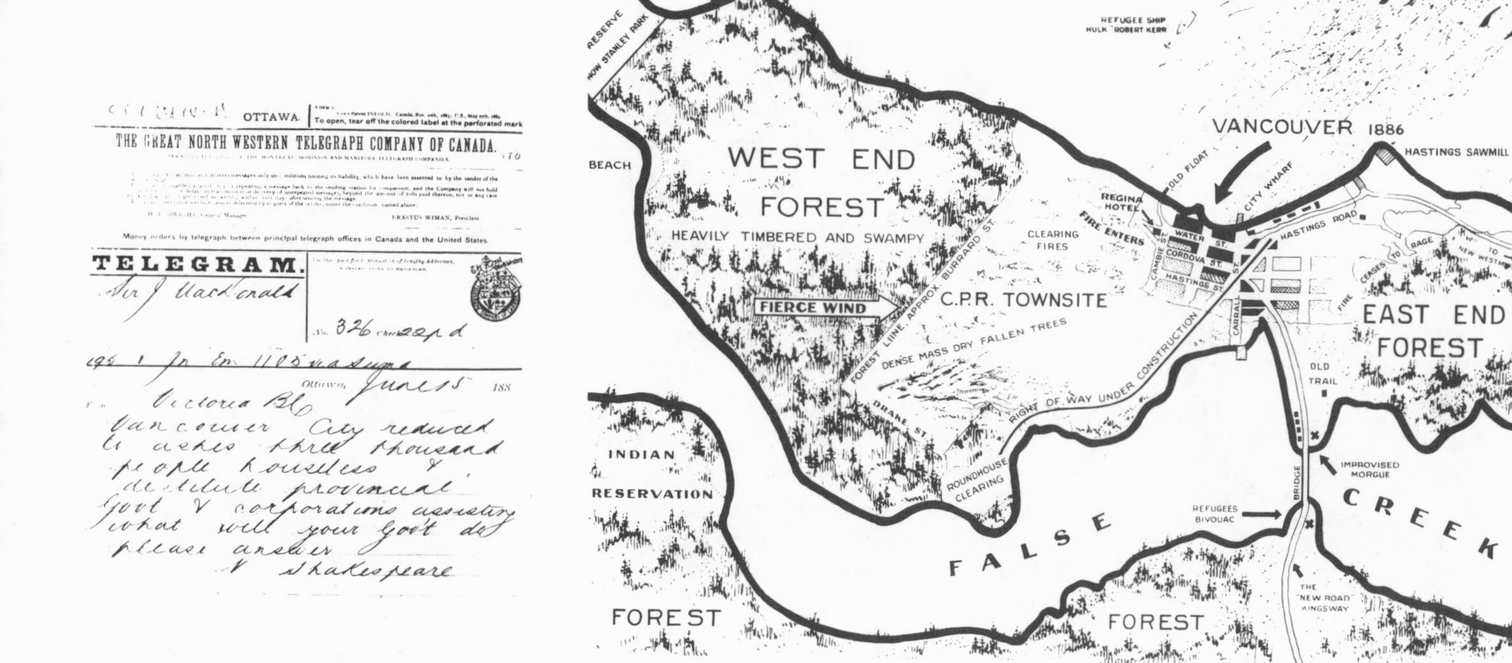
OTTAWA.

To open, tear off the colored label at the perforated mark

THE GREAT NORTH WESTERN TELEGRAPH COMPANY OF CANADA.

ERASTUS WIMAN, President.

Money orders by telegraph between principal telegraph offices in Canada and the United States.

TELEGRAM.

Sir J MacDonald

No. 326 ch 22 pd

Ottawa, June 15 188

Victoria BC

Vancouver City reduced to ashes three thousand people houseless & destitute provincial Govt & corporations assisting what will your Govt do please answer

N Shakespeare

Telegram from Victoria M.P. Noah Shakespeare reported Vancouver "reduced to ashes."

Major J.S. Matthews's map details the progress of the "great Vancouver fire." A watcher from a boat described the scene as a "grand but awful sight." The city was soon rebuilt on a larger scale.

The aristocratic Henry Glynne Fiennes-Clinton —"a typical Anglican, a finger in every pie."

In April, 1886, the City of Vancouver was incorporated. Two months later, it burned to the ground. It was a Sunday, the day of Pentecost, when the fire struck, and it was Father Clinton of St. James's who saw the pillar of smoke and rang the church bell. "It was just the Sunday school hour," he said. "I soon had the frightened children in a place of safety, but nothing could stop that fire. Like a great cyclone of flame, it swept the town. . . ." Father Clinton burned the soles off his shoes. Standing waist-deep in Burrard Inlet, a child clutched to his shoulders, his congregation around him, he watched the village smolder.

Father Henry Glynne Fiennes-Clinton had come to the diocese in 1884 as a missionary to the Thompson River Indians. The aristocratic high churchman – a member of the family of the Dukes of Newcastle, a graduate of Oxford's Keble College and the former principal of Bishop's College, Calcutta – had expected to stay here for a year. He stayed until 1912. He liked to say that he had no choice – his money was lost in the fire.

"Fiennes-Clinton was a typical Anglican," says Archbishop Godfrey Gower, "a finger in every pie." He conducted a school for boys and kept wicket for the Vancouver cricket side. ("Mind I see you in church tomorrow!" he would hiss in a batsman's ear as the ball was bowled.) He built the community's first hospital, St. Luke's, and brought Sister Frances Redmond from Eastern Canada to be matron and director of a school for nurses. Father Clinton was a member of the Vancouver Amateur Fire Brigade and ran with the boys who drew the hose wagon (and won the world championship in Tacoma). He helped organize a public library and was chairman on the evening that members of the Vancouver Reading Room decided to repeal the by-law restricting "the privileges of the reading room to persons of the male sex only." Missions to Seamen began, says Godfrey Gower, with Fiennes-Clinton recognizing "the loneliness, the temptation, the lack of spiritual ministration" to the sailors docked along the waterfront near his church. He rebuilt St. James's after the great fire and he built two mission churches in Vancouver: St. Michael's on Mount Pleasant and St. Paul's in the West End. He was, said a later St. James's priest, Father Wilberforce Cooper, "the spiritual father of Vancouver."

The forms of worship at St. James's were and are marked by ritual formal, austere and splendid (it must be one of the few parishes which still crown a May Queen in honor of Our Lady). This was exactly what Bishop Sillitoe – "a *moderate* high churchman" – liked, but he recognized a need for services of another style. So did Father Clinton, who chaired a meeting at which it was determined to form a church "which was distinctively to uphold the principles of the Reformation and of the Evangelical Ministry." A group of churchgoers, many from Father Clinton's parish, began holding meetings in 1888 in a Miss Wales's schoolroom on Seymour Street. In August, land was bought from the CPR, and in 1889, the first service was held in what the townspeople called "the old Root House" and subsequently became Christ Church Cathedral.

The first rector, the Reverend H.P. Hobson, satisfied the bishop's requirements that he be a "low churchman." Hobson was a graduate of Wycliffe College, Toronto (with which Christ Church has continued to be associated, indirectly and sporadically, while the roots of St. James's are in Keble College and Toronto's Trinity).

Pioneer Cricket Club, 1890, posed in front of what appear to be the Pearly Gates. Father Pat is fourth from left, back. A moustachioed Father Clinton is second from right, front.

Hobson opened a school for the Chinese in Vancouver. There is a photograph of the young rector, looking like a bare-knuckles pugilist, surrounded by several coolie candidates for baptism.

Sillitoe, who loved the Indians, had a remarkable lack of affection for the Chinese. "The Chinese are most undesirable," he told the Royal Colonial Institute on a trip to London. "I would give anything to see the last Chinaman pass clean out of British Columbia."

If this attitude was untypical of Sillitoe, it was entirely typical of the anti-Oriental prejudice of the time. "Let this new empire be for our own race," declared John Robson, editor of the New Westminster *British Columbian*, while Victoria's *British Colonist*, founded by Amor de Cosmos, published editorials about "the Chinese Evil." Robson and de Cosmos each served a term as premier of the province. Even Sir John A. MacDonald, the country's favorite father figure, said, "It is not advantageous to the country that the Chinese should come and settle in Canada, producing a mongrel race. . . ."

White hatred had broken loose wherever Chinese workers went – Australia, California, the Cariboo gold fields – and the basic reason was fear: that the Chinese would monopolize the labor market, make a great deal of money and take it back to China, or stay and overwhelm the new land.

The Knights of Labor was one group of workers which campaigned against the Chinese; but the savage antagonism toward them ran throughout society, and was manifested in acts from street marches and riots to discriminatory legislation. In 1887, the Vancouver Vigilance Committee distributed this message: "Due notice is hereby given warning all Chinamen to move. . .from. . . the City of Vancouver on or before the 15th day of June. . .failing which all Chinamen. . . shall be forceably expelled. . . ." One of the committee's first targets was John McDougall, who had hired Chinese men to clear land. McDougall's workers were forced onto a boat for Victoria. "I can see the picture yet," said George H. Keefer, "poor Chinks with their rice sacks and big balancing poles, all heading for the wharf; they were coming out of the blackened timber and brush from all directions, and some of them were coming on the toe of a boot."

Not everyone felt this way; many women found it convenient to have Chinese servants ("by this time we had a Chinaman," wrote the mistress of St. Mary's Mount) and some had more generous attitudes than that. But the antagonistic feeling was dominant enough to make British Columbia an uncomfortable place for the Chinese to be.

In Farwell (later Revelstoke), where the principal trade was whisky selling, Violet Sillitoe saw a river shanty burn. "The night was calm, no wind was blowing," she wrote, "so the fire burnt itself out. . .no attempt being made to put it out. 'It's only a Chinaman's; let it burn,' I heard one white man say; though the agonized cry of the poor Celestial with his house on fire was dreadful to hear."

And yet, despite the community's destestation of the Chinese, the bishop wanted to offer them something. "Our responsibilities toward these heathen sojourners are in no wise diminished," he wrote. "There are about seven or eight thousand of them in our midst, and no endeavour whatever is made to evangelize them. I have again applied to the SPG on their behalf, but even without this aid I feel that something must be done. A native Chinese missionary, at present working in San Francisco, has offered himself to me, but an engagement with him will involve the responsibility of

H.P. Hobson, first rector of Christ Church, Vancouver, and a baptismal class, circa 1890. Missions to the Chinese were the work of a few clergymen and a number of devoted Church women. Hobson's mission became the Church of the Good Shepherd, a leading Vancouver parish.

To all and Singular to whome these Presents shall come
Acton Windeyer by Divine Permission Bishop of New Westminster, Greeting
Know ye that We the said Bishop of New Westminster for and in consideration of the diligence, good life and sincere religion of our beloved in Christ Henry Irwin Priest have admitted constituted and appointed and by these Presents do admit constitute and appoint him the said Henry Irwin one of our domestic Chaplains to serve us in the performance of the Divine Offices within our house or chapel and wheresoever else we may from time to time appoint him thereto
In Testimony Whereof we have put our Seal, which we use in this case, to these Presents and have subscribed the same this twenty fifth day of October in the year of Our Lord One thousand eight hundred and ninety and of our consecration the Eleventh

"AW New Westminster" (L.S.)

J Pelly
Registrar.

Father Pat's appointment, noted by Sillitoe's father-in-law, diocesan registrar Justinian Pelly.

$930 or $1000 a year. I am still considering whether to incur this obligation."

Many Church of England members in British Columbia felt a less ambivalent concern for the Chinese. John Sheepshanks had instructed a Chinese group in New Westminster, as had a Chinese-speaking lay missionary named Henry Reeve in Yale. In the Sillitoe years, Ten Yong, a Chinese lay catechist, came from Honolulu to work out of Hobson's mission (which became the Church of the Good Shepherd).

Another worker from Honolulu was the Reverend Herbert Gowen. Gowen (who was to be the chronicler of Sillitoe's episcopate) opened a school for Chinese men and boys, with support from the CMS. The Chinese Mission Aid Association was formed to assist diocesan work among the Chinese. The clergy of Christ Church and St. Paul's were prominent in this work, along with what Frank Peake described as "a number of enthusiastic women."

Gowen called work among the Chinese "slow and difficult. . . .there was, perhaps, on their part no consciousness of the need for mission work. . .nor was there any great enthusiasm among the Church people of the diocese on behalf of a mission. Rather, sad it is to say, there was a sort of unchristian conviction that such a mission was a mistake and needless waste of money. Nevertheless, upon the Bishop's heart, the responsibility weighed heavily, and he was glad indeed to find someone ready to take up the work."

In 1889, Bishop Sillitoe installed himself as rector of Holy Trinity, a posting made partly through financial need. His curate was Father Pat.

Father Pat was now the husband of pretty Fanny Innes, daughter of the head of Her Majesty's Naval Establishment at Esquimalt. They had met at Donald, and were, said Violet Sillitoe, "like two children in the delight they took in everything, in the pride they took in each other and their cosy little home." Their life together, their "unclouded happiness," lasted about a year. Shortly after birth, their child died, and, three days later, Fanny followed. The evening of the funeral, Father Pat moved into the Sillitoes' house.

Bishop Sillitoe often travelled a great distance to take a church service, only to discover, on opening his mouth to speak, that he had no voice. On two successive Sundays at Yale, no words would come; on the third, wrote Violet, he was able to preach. The sermon text: "And the Lord opened the mouth of the ass."

The bishop's eyes, at this time, had a look of perpetual surprise; and, while he undoubtedly was frequently surprised, the protuberance was more likely evidence of an exopthalmic goiter. It was, probably, an enlarged thyroid, pressing against the larynx, which prevented speech, while Sillitoe's extraordinary energy may have been the result of a heightened metabolic rate produced by the endocrine disturbance.

His voice, happily, did not desert him on the day at Osoyoos when he preached to General William Sherman and his cavalry escort. (What did he tell the burner of Atlanta? Hell is war?)

Bishop's household: Sing, Gin, Father Pat, dogs Piper, Grip and Jingo. Pat was "a charming member of the family," wrote Violet, "the love between him and the Bishop that of father and son."

"The Root House" was the name locals gave the future Christ Church Cathedral in 1889. Built to "uphold the principles of the Reformation and Evangelical Ministry," it became the "extreme low church," providing an alternative to the Anglo-Catholic ceremonies of Sillitoe and Clinton.

A Sunday-school picnic for the children of Christ Church, Vancouver, in 1892. Teaching, says Dr. Hilda Hellaby, was "very good and very thorough. I practically knew the New Testament by heart." Some of these picnickers may now be nonagenarian parishioners in the diocese.

Synod of the Diocese of New Westminster, 1890—year of the Winnipeg Conference, a preparation for the first General Synod. Only two delegates from the Pacific Coast attended the conference: Archdeacon Woods and CPR engineer Lacey R. Johnson, a prominent Vancouver layman.

On the tenth anniversary of Bishop Sillitoe's consecration, he looked at the decade of work (and a recent increase in funds – Christ Church, Vancouver raised $7,000 in one year) and preached at Holy Trinity: "Of myself, I can do nothing." People of New Westminster honored the Sillitoes at a reception in the Opera House.

1892. There was a new bishop in Victoria. George Hills had retired, to be replaced by the Reverend William Wilcox Perrin of Southampton. Now, his wife gone, the founder of the Church of England in British Columbia left to spend his last years in a country parish in Norwich, where the bishop – appointed to the office by Queen Victoria for his work in New Westminster – was John Sheepshanks.

That year, Holy Trinity was declared Cathedral Church of the Diocese of New Westminster. On the Feast of the Circumcision, 1892, Acton Sillitoe was enthroned.

Now Sillitoe was about to take on one of his greatest tasks: the bringing together of mutually suspicious bishops at the first Canadian General Synod.

As early as 1881, Sillitoe had written: "I venture to look forward to the day when besides the great confederation which joins together politically the various provinces of the Dominion, there will be a confederation, too, of the Church of England in Canada, joined together in the unity of the spirit and by the bond of peace, and strengthened in her work by the happy realization of the fundamental truth that we are 'all of us members one of another,' living stones of one temple built upon 'the faith once delivered to the saints.'"

In 1890, he had attended the Winnipeg Conference, which established the structure for a General Synod, to meet in Toronto on the second Wednesday of September, 1893.

The 53-year-old bishop was not well. In 1892, he had suffered a violent attack of influenza and had not entirely recovered when he set out on a physically devastating three-month speaking tour of Eastern Canada. He returned from the east with pneumonia.

Six days before the synod was to open, he wrote to the Rev. Herbert Mogg, compiler of the *Monthly Record*, the journal of the Diocese of New Westminster Home Committee in England: "My Dear Mogg: This year has been quite the most trying of my episcopate. . . .I came home a wreck. That God granted me recovery is, I venture to hope, a sign that my work for Him is not yet done."

On September 13, 1893, delegates to the first General Synod of the Church of England in Canada gathered in worship at St. Alban's Cathedral, Toronto. Among them were the Reverend H.G. Fiennes-Clinton from St. James's and two men who were to play important roles in the development of the New Westminster diocese: the Reverend Canon E.S.W. Pentreath of Winnipeg and the Reverend A.U. de Pencier, priest-vicar of St. Alban's.

The delegates moved to the Convocation Hall of Trinity College for their meetings. There were four distinct groups among them: the CMS Evangelicals from Rupertsland; the United Empire Loyalists and Church of Ireland stalwarts from Ontario; the staunch, traditional Maritimers; and the British Columbia mavericks. There were tensions between high and low churchmen and major differences between delegates from the synods of Rupertsland and 'Canada.' Acton Sillitoe, representing an independent diocese, was a reconciling force among them, working with Travers Lewis of Ontario, senior bishop in 'Canada,' and Robert Machray of Rupertsland, who was elected Primate.

"Well do I recall," said Nova Scotia Bishop Frederick Courtney, "his strenuous endeavour to avoid not only the impending deadlock, but the threatened failure to consummate the consolidation of the Church. . .it was largely owing to his pleading with his fellow Bishops, and his advocacy of a conciliatory attitude. . .that harmony was restored, and peace came to cement and perfect our union."

When the Solemn Declaration was eventually signed, Bishop Sillitoe was asked to preach at a service of thanksgiving. "The Canadian General Synod," says Godfrey Gower, "is a monument to Bishop Sillitoe."

Christ Church Boys' Brigade on old Court House steps in 1890. Commander of the group was Captain Lacey Johnson (front row, with stick). Mrs. Johnson and church ladies made uniforms.

Palm Sunday, 1894. Bishop Sillitoe, ill after an overnight journey from Kamloops, preached in his cathedral. Later that morning, he drove to St. Paul's for a confirmation service. After the laying on of hands, he broke down in the West End church.

The bishop was forced to stay in bed until after Easter. Then, wrote Henry Edwardes, "he came to Lytton, which place he always loved, despite its evil winds, hoping to build up his health again, but day by day we could see there was no improvement, and that he was growing weaker and more nervous and sleepless."

On May 5, the bishop went to Vancouver for more confirmations. "He returned to Lytton," wrote Edwardes, "decidedly worse. A number of Indians had been prepared for Confirmation, and so again he braced himself up to give them the precious Gift. On Whit Sunday we had all ready for him at the Indian Church by 8:50 a.m., when he came to the door supported by Mrs. Sillitoe. The Indian churchwardens and sidesmen received him, and the big congregation rose as he entered. It was a touching and anxious service for all of us, a service full of self-sacrifice. . .he could hardly get through it."

Bishop Sillitoe was taken to Yale, sick and sleepless. "O God, help me!" he cried. On May 27, he sank into delirium. An old friend, Dr. Hanington, came from Victoria. June 1, the bishop seemed improved enough for travel. The Fraser was in flood, so he was carried to a steamer at Ruby Creek for the journey to New Westminster.

His condition grew worse. He whispered prayers and read music scores. A prayer vigil began at churches. A Vancouver newspaper, *The World,* scolded the illness, as though editorial support was what the bishop needed. "The cutting short of so useful a career," it wrote, "would be deplorable."

The doctor told the bishop there was no hope, the infection could not be stopped. "My poor little wife," said Acton. "This comes very hard on you."

The bishop's chaplain, the Reverend C. Croucher, gave him Holy Communion. The bishop said he hoped he had left the affairs of the diocese "fairly in order." Then the delirium returned ("Papa, pour some more hot water in; make the ocean not so cold"?) June 9, it ended. The telegram to England said: "Bishop asleep."

"Bishop Sillitoe developed a church," says Godfrey Gower, "which showed its concern for every facet of society." Certainly Sillitoe's work and interests were extraordinarily wide-ranging, including general education (an advocate in 1890 of a British Columbia university, he was chairman of its first meeting of Convocation), industry, politics, the arts and civic development (he was responsible for the laying of sidewalks in New Westminster).

"The last church built in Vancouver during my husband's episcopate," wrote Violet Sillitoe, "was St. Luke's, River Road. Other churches built during my husband's time were All Saints', Ladner; St. Alban's, Ashcroft; Christ Church, Surrey Centre; St. Alban's, Langley Prairie; St. Paul's, Kamloops; Nelson; Balfour; St. Barnabas', New Westminster; Enderby; Armstrong; Vernon; and Penticton, and many little Indian churches." She had forgotten St. James's, St. Paul's, St. Michael's and Christ Church in Vancouver and St. Peter's in Donald. Other parishes in the diocese included St. Thomas's, Chilliwack; St. John's, Yale; St. Paul's, Lytton; St. Saviour's, Cariboo; St. Mary the Virgin, Sapperton, and Holy Trinity Cathedral, New Westminster.

Sunday, June 10, the celebrated bells of that cathedral tolled for the Bishop of New

Vancouver in the 1890s, when the West End was the most fashionable section of the city, filling up with mansions of CPR executives, lucky prospectors and wealthy tradesmen. A horse-drawn wagon moves west along Georgia Street towards Christ Church, which can be seen at far left.

Westminster.

Henry Edwardes and Richard Small wrote: "Bishop Sillitoe was exactly the man needed for such a country as British Columbia, and to influence for good the lives of those adventurous spirits who, in rough days, had left the old country to begin life afresh in the far West, under new conditions and with new prospects."

The Lytton Indian congregation sent a message to Mrs. Sillitoe: "The Indians very sorry because the Bishop is die, because he loves them very much and takes care of them. . .they all feel they belong to him. From today they will pray all the time for his happiness in Paradise."

"The offer of the Bishopric of New Westminster," wrote Herbert Gowen, had "seemed to upset all [Sillitoe's] plans and to make a radical change in the whole outlook of his life." And perhaps he would have preferred to remain in the diplomatic circles of Darmstadt and Geneva, sipping cordials and attending musicales. But then he never would have ridden over a canyon on a handcar, never have heard the silver hit the stage while he played the accordion in Theatre Royal.

There were those who thought he had made a great sacrifice; that, had he stayed in England, he might have won the archbishopric of York or even Canterbury. Perhaps he did better than that. Lying beneath his Celtic cross, lofted by the prayers of the Lytton Indians, he won, perhaps, Paradise.

Celtic cross marks hillside grave of Acton Sillitoe above the Fraser in New Westminster.

IN MEMORY OF LIEUT. HAROLD HEBER OWEN.

Part II

The Scholar, the Soldier, and the Grand Old Man

Religious history is very different
to what men often wish it to be.
–John Dart

John Dart, Bishop of New Westminster 1895-1910. His charge included Cariboo and "Coutney."

John Dart was not elected second Bishop of New Westminster. He was not even nominated for election. October 3, 1894, an electoral synod met in Holy Trinity Cathedral and considered six candidates: the Reverend H.H. Mogg, once a priest in the diocese, now vicar of Chittoe, Chippenham, England, and editor of the Home Committee's *Monthly Record;* the Reverend W. Hibbert Binney, son of the late Bishop of Nova Scotia, and vicar of Wilton, Cheshire; the Reverend J. Cope of St. Thomas, Ontario; the Reverend Dr. Langtry of Toronto, Ontario; Canon George Thornloe of Sherbrooke, Quebec; and the Reverend Daniel Stine, principal of the Dorchester Missionary College, England. Mr. Binney was declared bishop, with thirteen votes to Canon Thornloe's five.

Mr. Binney said thank you, no.

February 20, 1895, the synod electors met again and went through fourteen ballots without giving any candidate the two-thirds majority required for election. (When the voting was abandoned, Mogg was in the lead.)

And so, Bishops Perrin (British Columbia) and Ridley (Caledonia), acting at the request of diocesan synod, which had every reason to say "What now, m'Lords?", consulted the Archbishop of Canterbury ("What now, your Grace?"). The Archbishop talked with the Bishops of London, St. Alban's and Norwich (John Sheepshanks) and the choice was made: Canon John Dart, organizing secretary in the Diocese of Manchester for the Society for the Propagation of the Gospel. On St. Peter's Day in St. Paul's Cathedral, John Dart became John New Westminster.

Dart, Devonshire born, had a Don Quixote look – gaunt, deep-eyed, his long face ending in a whiskered point. He was 58 years old, with a long scholarly and missionary career behind him. After taking honors in law at Oxford, he had served as vice-principal and lecturer in science at St. Peter's College, Peterborough, England, and as president of King's University, Windsor, Nova Scotia. Ordained by Bishop Claughton of Colombo, he was the bishop's chaplain in Ceylon and warden of St. Thomas's College. He was made Canon of Halifax by Bishop Herbert Binney. (Dart's third son was given the same Christian name – Hibbert – as Binney's son.) In 1883, Dart wrote *A Companion to the Prayer Book Psalter.* In 1885, he returned to England to work for the SPG. Ten years later, August 19, 1895, he, his wife and their four sons arrived in New Westminster.

"It is," he wrote, "a magnificent country,

as large as France, with a healthy climate, destined, in all probability, to become at no very distant date the home of a great English nation. It depends greatly upon us to determine what the character of that nation shall be. We are now laying the foundations. God grant that we may lay them and build upon them wisely and well!"

But Dart found his diocese in critical condition. Nineteen clergymen, divided, dispirited, worked its 186,000 square miles. There was economic depression in New Westminster, and the diocesan endowment fund, invested in real estate, produced no income. "I want our English friends to know," wrote the new bishop, "that our finances are in a very bad state; in fact, we have not enough to pay our missionaries even the very small stipends that have been promised to them."

The diocese swept north from the 49th Parallel through the Fraser, Upper Columbia and Thompson Valleys, the Cariboo and the Kootenays. "From all of these places," wrote Bishop Dart, "appeals have come to me. . .I am utterly unable to respond."

"My Lord," began one of these appeals, "I am taking the liberty of addressing you in the interests of the members of the English Church living in this, the Cariboo District. At present we are entirely without any Church service, although there are many members of the English Communion in Quesnelle, Barkerville, and at various points along the Cariboo waggon road. Some years ago there was a resident Church of England clergyman here – a Mr. Brooks – and the consequence is that all the children have been christened by him. . . .Since then, with the exception of an occasional itinerant Methodist or Presbyterian preacher, this country has been entirely without spiritual advice. If your Lordship can find some means of giving us the benefit of the Church Service, you will be conferring a great boon upon us all. I might say that the weekly collections, if services were held, would amount to about twenty dollars ($20) a month at Quesnelle." The letter was signed "Your obedient servant, Richard H. Parkinson."

"There is no lack of clergy willing to work in New Westminster," Dart told the New Westminster Missionary Society he had organized. "Numbers of good men in the States and from different parts of Canada would come here if I could guarantee them living salaries. . . .If I had an additional £800 a year I would send four men before Christmas into the new mining districts."

Mrs. Dart, first honorary president of the Diocesan Board of the Woman's Auxiliary (1904).

House of Bishops at the second General Synod of the Anglican Church of Canada, held in 1896 at St. John's College, Winnipeg. Archbishop Robert Machray, first Primate of All Canada, is seated fourth from left. John New Westminster stands almost directly behind him, sixth from left.

In New Westminster, the scholar-bishop addressed his people on religion and science, textual variations in Biblical manuscripts, Hebrew tradition and ancient monuments, church doctrines and the duties of the laity as "the guardians of public worship."

But Dart was more than an empurpled pedagogue. "I am now in the Kootenay mining country," he wrote, "where the mountains are said to be teeming with silver and lead [and] towns are rising like magic amidst dense forests.

"During the last fortnight I have had the novel, but not unpleasing, experience of taking meals in railway and mining camps, and sleeping in rough wayside places. Occasionally, where the line is unfinished, I have had to scramble down a trail along a steep mountainside. I am greatly comforted at finding that my legs hold out rather better than the young cleric's who is going round with me. But it is hard upon breeches and gaiters! I am hoping to get into New Westminster by night and change my clothes before my wife sees me."

Excerpts from Dart's diary: "September 26–Confirmation of Indians at Lytton. Mr. Small's incessant and self-denying work has produced good results. Nothing can exceed the reverent demeanour of the Indians in Divine Service. After Service. . .the usual palaver and ceremony of shaking hands." "October 5–Consecrated the church at Kelowna in the name of St. Michael and All Angels." "November 24–By train to Mission City. Held Service in the Store, which is fitted up as a temporary church. Large congregation."

"We came last night," he wrote, "from the Three Forks, partly in the train and partly walking, as the line is not yet finished. There was a body on board, enclosed in a rough pine coffin. It was a miner who had died from overwork and exposure in a wet mine, and his comrades asked me to bury him. We stopped about a mile from New Denver, and walked in a narrow trail over tree-stumps through the dense forest by the dim light of lanterns. It was a strange scene. The lanterns just showed a score or so of rugged men around the grave amongst the trees, and the women standing by. The poor fellows seemed grateful out of all proportion to the service I had done, but I understood it. However reckless their lives, they hate the idea of being buried 'like a dog.'"

In 1894, Henry Irwin – Father Pat – had returned to Ireland. Now, from Mount Kennedy, he wrote to Bishop Dart, and was asked to be mission priest at Rossland. Father Pat was back in the Diocese of New Westminster in January, 1896. "Mr. Irwin is making a real venture of faith," wrote the bishop. "He pays all his expenses out, I am not able to guarantee him a dollar of salary, and his maintenance (he looks for no more than a bare livelihood) will depend entirely upon his acceptableness to the rough untaught people amongst whom he will be thrown."

The rough untaught people liked the tough Irishman. George Winteler, who composed Service-able verse as "The Prospector," wrote:

We don't go much on parsons,
Here in the minin' belt
'Tween Rossland and the Similkameen;
But there was one we felt
A most uncommon likin' for –
You take my word for that;
The latch-string hung outside each door
For good friend Father Pat.

"He was best," said Frances McNab, "when he sat in the open doorway of [his] shack. The shack. . .was always open."

Bartlett's Pack Train at Sandon, a Kootenay town full of miners in the 1890s, now full of ghosts.

"My experience," said Father Pat, "is that the more you trust human nature and treat people like human beings, and not with suspicion, the better you will like them. If I knew a man was a born thief, I would throw the doors open to him and trust him just the same, relying on his better nature not to betray me."

J.G. Thynne remembered a church service conducted by his father, Canon Thynne, and attended by Father Pat. "One old fellow with a pack on his back shakes hands and says, 'Put her there, Old Man! I'll be damned if you ain't a damned good sport! Come and have a shot with me, and bring that Sky Pilot chum of yours. All you boys, belly up to the bar!' I don't know whether my father imbibed or not," continued Thynne, "but I guess Father Pat did, as he seldom refused."

"He was a very poor preacher," wrote Desmond Catchpole, who learned the Father Pat stories as Archdeacon of Kootenay, "but had the reputation of being willing to do good wherever he might. . .no matter who the person might be. There were a good many loose women there in those days, and the old undertaker told me that Father Pat said to him that when any of these died or committed suicide, he would be willing to bury them, if no one else would."

He wore the Church of England brand,
But didn't bank on creeds;
His way to hearts was not with words,
But helpin', lovin' deeds.
Though we were hard to work upon,
Nor readily enticed,
We called him the first Christian
That ever lived, since Christ.

Father Pat, recalled a Rossland settler, "was all over the country, holding services and laying the foundations of a church at Trail, and at Grand Forks and other points in the Boundary, the nearest. . .forty miles over the mountains west of Rossland – two days' journey for most men, up and down steep trails, but only one day's for Father Pat, whether on foot or in the saddle."

Fred J. Smyth of the *Cranbrook Courier* saw the red-whiskered priest striding along the street at Moyie one day in 1898. Father Pat, in turtleneck sweater, overalls and hob-nailed boots, had just walked from Kuska-nook, about fifty miles distance.

It was all his territory, and so was the Diocese of Spokane, Washington, when he wanted it to be. He told friends he was "licensed by the American Bishop as well as our own, so that I can pray for the President now and then when I've a foot across the line."

Anne Mercier, in her 1909 *Father Pat: A Hero of the Far West,* told of a saloon girl the priest had helped to reform: "A man meeting her in the hotel greeted her with insulting words. Father Pat happened to be there, and, with his fist in the fellow's face, said: 'You scoundrel, get out of this very quick, or I'll help you out.' The man speedily vanished, for the Padre's skill as a boxer was well known."

But the pugilist priest didn't win them all. One Saturday night, coming back from a football game in Nelson, he wore his hat tipped forward, almost but not quite covering two black eyes.

"I just stood and looked at him," said a miner friend, "and Father Pat said. . .'What's the matter with you? Can't you speak to a man?'

"'I was just thinking,' said I, 'What a pretty pair of eyes those are. Prettiest I ever saw.'

"'It's not the first time,' growled the priest.

"'Well,' said I, 'you're a nice one for a minister. You're not going to preach with eyes like that?'

"'Wouldn't be the first time for that, either,' said Father Pat."

"Father Pat no preacher?" said an old Kootenay hand. "Well, I guess he was. There was a young fellow down at Trail very ill. The doctors said there was no salvation for him, he'd got to die; so they sent for Father Pat. He talked to him a bit, and the young chap felt better, and held out his hand and said, 'Thank you, Father Pat. Goodbye.'

"'Goodbye?' said Father Pat. 'Goodbye? What do you mean by that? Do you think I'm goin' anywhere else but you? I'll say goodnight to you if you like; at Doomsday, I'll say good mornin'! It's only over the other side of the Divide, and we'll meet together there!'

"The boy died easy."

Railways were opening up the province. The population of the Kootenays was already swelling in 1899 and the next year the Crow's Nest line would cut through to Kootenay Lake, bringing more settlers west from Calgary. Clergy and laity of the area wrote New Westminster Synod, suggesting creation of a new Diocese of Kootenay. November 8, 1899, Synod recommended that the Diocese of New Westminster be divided at the 120th Meridian, and that the division take place immediately. The new diocese would remain, however, under the authority of the Bishop of New Westminster until Kootenay's bishopric endowment fund reached $40,000. And so Kootenay remained under New Westminster's supervision until 1914.

In 1900, with Rossland established, Father Pat asked Bishop Dart to send him to some new, unopened country. The Irish priest was seriously overworked, and the bishop offered him a lighter posting. But Father Pat insisted, and he was sent to the South Okanagan. A year later, his health broken, he allowed the bishop to send him home to Ireland to rest.

Father Pat took the train east; but outside Montreal, he got off and began to walk the Sault Recollet Road. A farmer found him in the snow, his feet so badly frozen the boots had to be cut away. In Notre Dame Hospital, he charmed the Sisters, but would give no name except "William Henry." He gave the resident, Dr. Kingston, his papers and some letters to friends, but demanded secrecy. January 13, 1902, Father Pat died. He was 43 years old.

They brought Father Pat's body back and

Morning after the great New Westminster fire of 1898. Women of Holy Trinity Cathedral examine the church's treasured bells cooling in the rubble enclosed by "an outline in bare stone."

buried it beside Fanny and her baby in Sapperton Cemetery. In Rossland, they built a monument. One of the inscriptions is "I was thirsty, and ye gave me drink."

He died; we built a monument
At Rossland, on the hill,
And many sun-burned prospectors
Chipped in to pay the bill.
And when I look upon it
A great big teardrop starts;
But it's nothing to the monument
He built within our hearts.

Beside the date Sunday, September 11, 1898, the parish register of Holy Trinity Cathedral reports: "There was no service today. The disastrous fire of last night and this morning destroyed our Cathedral. . ."

"Fire broke out about 11:30 p.m. at the warehouse of Brackman and Ker," wrote Leslie Pearson, a Holy Trinity rector of the 1950s. "The shingled roof had been ignited from sparks sent out from the funnel of the river steamer *Edgar.* The fire was soon out of control, the flames spreading eastward toward the public market, leaping across

Front Street. The flames set fire to the steamers *Gladys* and *Bon Accord.* These. . . loosened from their moorings. . .their ropes burned, floated down the waterfront, setting fire to everything in their course. A strong southeast wind sprang up. Soon the whole city. . .was a raging inferno."

Sunday morning, "nothing was left but a chaos of ruin and destruction." The cathedral was "an outline in bare stone." The rector, the Reverend Alfred Shildrick, had piled the church records, sacred vessels, altar cross, candlesticks and lectern into a wheelbarrow and trundled them to safety.

Bishop Dart was in Halifax, preparing to leave for England. The burned-out congregation was not comforted by his message: "The Diocese. . .should now look forward to a Cathedral that would be a credit to it. . . not a mere appendage to a Parish Church." Holy Trinity, however, was restored (with assistance from Mrs. Sillitoe; its interior modelled after St. Paul's, Kensington) and, in 1902, re-consecrated as the cathedral of the diocese. But Bishop Dart held his diocesan executive meetings in Vancouver.

St. Paul's Church, originally a mission in the CPR False Creek community called Yaletown, about to be moved, in 1898, to the West End of Vancouver. Canon Harold Underhill was rector.

Vancouver, at the turn of the century, had a population of 27,000 and was the economic centre of British Columbia. By 1904, Eastern Canadian and European investments would begin the province's large-scale lumber, mining and fishing industries. The little sawmill clearing on the edge of Burrard Inlet was getting ready to become a metropolis.

Bishop Dart worried about "a prevalent and increasing danger – the secularizing of our daily life. The call to daily prayer is a reminder that money is not the chief good and that there is something of more importance even than business. . .I have spoken of our increasing need of new churches. I would now point out that we are expected to make greater use of our churches. . .than we generally do."

He warned that "all unnecessary labor and traffic must be strenuously resisted" on Sunday and he urged that religious education be provided in public schools. The bishop decried "evidence of increasing use of stimulating and intoxicating drugs," but the synod committee on temperance supported the Anglican Church's endorsement of "union and co-operation, on perfectly equal terms, between those who use and those who abstain from intoxicating drinks."

The anti-Oriental mood in Vancouver was growing uglier. The federal government, under Sir Wilfrid Laurier, had attempted to maintain a moderate bias against Oriental immigration, but that was insufficient for many British Columbians – niggardly trade unionists, xenophobic politicians and their toy press, and fanatic clergymen like the Reverend Dr. H.W. Fraser of Vancouver's First Presbyterian Church. "White Canada" was the cry, and a dozen anti-Oriental laws were passed; but they were not enough to stop the riots that were to come.

At Christ Church, where H.P. Hobson had conducted a mission school for Chinese immigrants, his successors as rector, L.N. Tucker and C.C. Owen, continued the work. Catechism classes for the Chinese were held in Bishop Dart's home. The Women's Auxiliary of Canada provided funds for "a building that would be a permanent centre of the work with a chapel for worship, a schoolroom for secular and religious teaching, and a lodging house for the catechists and converts." A Chinese Mission Building was opened on Homer Street in 1903. In charge of its work, under Owen's supervision, was the Reverend James Hau (whose name became, in the English community, "Hall.")

The first Japanese mission was begun in 1903 by Father Clinton, whose parish of St. James's included the Japanese quarter on Powell Street. Sister Kathleen O'Melia was the first missionary. In 1904, Bishop Dart appointed Gabriel Yosen Fujita as lay reader and missionary. Money for rent and books came from the St. James's branch of the Women's Auxiliary, presided over by Violet Sillitoe.

"Some of us may be opposed to the influx of Orientals," Bishop Dart told synod delegates. "But, however we may differ as citizens on this question, there can be only one opinion as to our duty as Christians toward the Orientals resident among us. We have to treat them with kindly consideration, equity and justice, and to remember that we are their debtors, holding in trust for them the blessings of the Gospel of Christ. What we have done for them so far is as nothing in comparison with what we ought to do."

The Women's Auxiliary of the diocese formed a Japanese Mission Committee and opened another mission, near the lumber mills in Vancouver's Holy Trinity parish.

September 7, 1907, the Asiatic Exclusion League, formed by the Vancouver Trades and Labor Council, mounted a parade. The city's newspapers urged their readers to attend. Finally, 30,000 people were crowded

Early twentieth century garden party at St. Luke's Home, Vancouver's first hospital, founded in 1890 by Father Clinton. Sister Frances Redmond (front row, white cuffs), who came from Eastern Canada to be matron and nursing school director, was honored by the city as "Best Citizen."

The *Laverock*, sailed by John Antle and his nine-year-old son from Vancouver to Alert Bay.

Newfoundlander John Antle, about 40, when he began the work of the Columbia Coast Mission.

around City Hall, at the edge of Chinatown and near what was called "Little Yokohama." The Reverend G.H. Wilson of St. Michael's begged the mob to act without violence. Small chance. The night ended with a riot of shop wrecking and beatings, as white thugs lurched through the Chinese and Japanese quarters. Police roped off the Oriental sections and imposed martial law. It remained in force ten days.

In 1904, Father Clinton's Seamen's Institute became part of the Flying Angel Mission, England's worldwide Missions to Seamen. And up the coast of British Columbia, Captain John Antle was setting the course of the Columbia Coast Mission.

John Antle was a Newfoundlander. His family had been cod fishermen, with a fleet of windjammers. At twelve years of age, it is said, he could box a compass and sail a yawl. Antle loved the sea, but he chose the priesthood. Ultimately, the two vocations were knotted together in his life.

Antle's first sea-borne mission was on the Atlantic, to the villages on Conception Bay. But in the late 1890s, he travelled west;

in 1899, he took charge of Fairview, the South Vancouver mission which became the parish of Holy Trinity.

The land held him four years. Then, he wrote, "One day some time in 1903, the little freight and passenger boat *Cassiar* steamed into the port of Vancouver from the logging camp route with four dead men on board. One man had bled to death in an open boat trying to reach. . .Vancouver. Another had died in his bunk for lack of surgical aid. To me, it was astounding. Four thousand men in the camps, working in one of the most dangerous callings in Canada, and the nearest doctor 50 to 350 miles away!

"What was to be done?" asked Antle. "Try to stir up the church, of course. This resulted in the formation of a joint committee of the Dioceses of Columbia and New Westminster. Go up, they said, and see if these things you tell us are really so, and here are a hundred dollars to finance the trip.

"I took the money and with it bought a three-quarter horsepower gas engine. It was a Springfield and its special cognomen was 'Bull Pup.' I installed it in the *Laverock* and on June 1, 1904, a memorable day,

Dr. W.A.B. Hutton, first ship's doctor. He was drowned in 1906 when the tug *Chehailus* on which he was travelling collided with the *Princess Victoria* in the First Narrows, Vancouver.

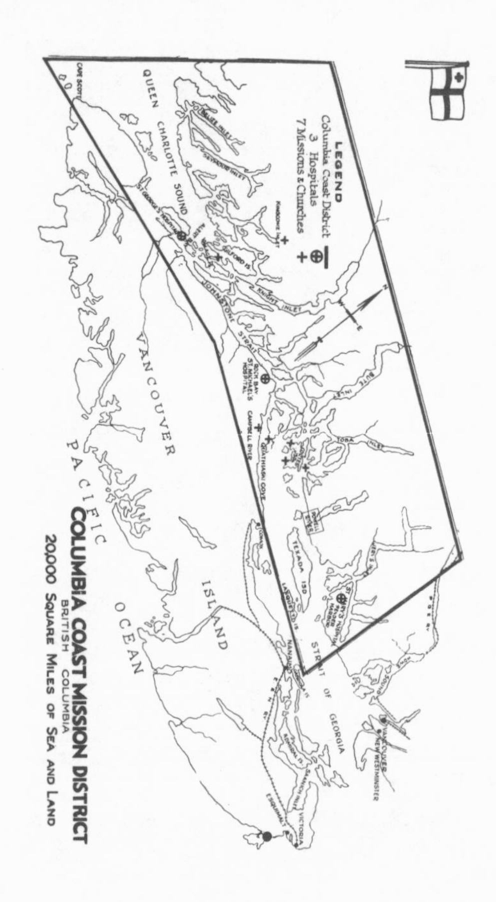

Antle's parish: 20,000 square miles of land and water, logging camps and Indian villages.

with my little son Vic, a lad of nine years, as crew, hoisted our sails, cranked the engine, and headed north by west in the sunlight."

Antle and his nine-year-old sailed their homemade 14-foot craft up the straits to Alert Bay on Cormorant Island, off the northeast edge of Vancouver Island. "They investigated every logging camp, fishing village and Indian reservation," writes Antle's daughter, Marion Antle Mennes, "the skipper oftentimes extracting a tooth, or baptizing a baby, or rendering some minor medical aid.

"John Antle," she explains, "was a somewhat amateur doctor."

Back in Vancouver, Antle told the two-diocese committee of the needs of the coast communities. "It's no good going up to a logger and preaching," he said. "We must demonstrate our Christianity in deeds."

The committee sent him to Montreal, to tell his story to the General Board of Missions. He came back with the grant Bishops Dart and Perrin had asked for: enough for half the cost of a floating hospital-chapel. In 1905, the 65-foot *Columbia* was launched, and so was the Columbia Coast Mission.

"The *Columbia*," writes Marion Antle Mennes, "was the first. . .combined church and medical mission to plough the coastal waters." Built by Wallace Shipyards at False Creek, Vancouver, "she was equipped with a built-in altar and a small organ. . .a surgery and doctor."

That same year, Antle and the Columbia Coast Mission, supported by the Hastings Mill Company, built Queen's Hospital at Rock Bay on Vancouver Island, near the company's logging operations. The Venerable Edwyn Pentreath, Archdeacon of Columbia, opened the hospital. The Victorian Order of Nurses provided furnishings and staff: Jean Sutherland, R.N., and Alice Franklin.

John Antle had his parish: 10,000 square miles of land and water, from the Gulf of Georgia to Queen Charlotte Sound. In the years ahead, he would build twelve churches and three hospitals.

"It would help us greatly," said John Dart, "if we had a theological college in British Columbia, instead of being entirely dependent upon the supply of men from a distance."

The bishop wanted a theological college for the province as early as 1899, and in 1902, Archdeacon Pentreath spoke of a Pacific Coast college to serve the province's dioceses. But it wasn't until 1905 that the money (as usual, from England) started to come. Mrs. Edward Tritton Gurney of Surrey, the widow of a Trinity College graduate, was the initial donor. Then Bishop Dart journeyed to England to raise more funds.

In 1908, a handsome endowment was provided for the establishment of a college by the New Westminster Association in England. The association had decided that a theological college would be a suitable memorial to the work of Bishop Hills. The founding bishop had died, aged 80, in 1895, in the vicarage at Parham. The fiftieth anniversary of his arrival in British Columbia was to be celebrated in 1909.

Patrons of the project included Princess Louise (perhaps recalling her ride in Bishop Sillitoe's buckboard); the Duchess of Marlborough; the Marquises of Salisbury, Normanby (Sillitoe's old friend) and Lansdowne; Baroness MacDonald; Lord Strathcona; Viscount Milner; and thirty-one bishops. Chairman of the committee was the Bishop of Norwich, the ubiquitous and Right Reverend John Sheepshanks, still a ramrod 6' 3", but looking now, with his long white beard, rather like Robert Crumb's Mr. Natural. (His granddaughter, he chuckled, "cried at the sight of me.") "I believe," said Sheepshanks, "I am the only one still living of the band of men who fifty years ago went forth from the Mansion House."

So now the money was promised, and Archdeacon Pentreath was able to secure land for a college. A name—St. Mark's—was selected by Mrs. Tritton Gurney.

St. Mark's, said Pentreath, would be "broad and comprehensive as the church itself. The West demands able and broad-minded men. . .men of breadth of vision and intellectual ability, loyal to their church, and able to deal effectively with the great problems confronting the church in this country."

The planned St. Mark's was not, however, broad and comprehensive enough for a group of Vancouver churchmen, led by

The Right Rev. John Sheepshanks, Bishop of Norwich, at the coronation of Edward VII.

Christ Church wedding, 1908. ("You'd look sweet upon the seat of a bicycle built for two.")

Christ Church rector C.C. Owen and his curate, A.H. Sovereign. Both were Wycliffe graduates, ergo "Evangelicals," and they had been stirred by the visit to the city of Isaac Stringer, the tough Wycliffe College missionary to the Eskimos, then Bishop of Yukon and later Archbishop of Rupertsland. (In 1909, when he was journeying from Fort McPherson to Dawson City, hunger forced him to eat his moccasins. "Soles better than tops," Stringer wrote in his diary.)

Christ Church was then, says Dr. Hilda Hellaby, "the extreme low church." In 1908, Hilda Hellaby was a student in the Christ Church Sunday School classes conducted by the Misses Seymour, Ruby and Adele. She heard Bishop Dart preach, and knew the "very fatherly" Cecil Owen. And she remembers that "the high church group used to call [Christ Church] 'St. Alms' Dish', because they had a collection plate propped up in the place where the cross is usually put."

It was, says Archdeacon Cecil Swanson, "a very different church from the present, although it was almost the same building. The Holy Table was devoid of any furnishings; no cross adorned it; a fine offertory plate stood in lonely isolation. . . .the ministers stood facing one another for the communion service. There was no clergy singing . . . .Let it be remembered that this type of worship was the norm in at least half the churches of Canada."

"Sir Charles Tupper and people of that age group who were the pillars of Christ Church. . .they'd turn in their graves if they saw it today," said Dr. Hellaby in 1979. "It was the extreme low church, the northwards position and all that. . . .These things took on a tremendous importance. Battles were waged over them."

And one battle was over the proposed theological college. Owen and Sovereign organized a group of Evangelicals at the home of H.J. Cambie. Concerned that two of the six dioceses in Western Canada were under "high church" influence and noting that money for St. Mark's was coming from SPG sources, they feared the college's teachings would be predominantly Anglo-Catholic and insufficiently Evangelical. The two Christ Church priests had already been giving informal instruction to young men considering entering the ministry. Now they began definite plans for a "Pacific Coast Theological College on Evangelical English lines" – clearly a Wycliffe of the West.

Money from England came for that, too; from the CMS and also from the Colonial and Continental Society.

A conference of Western Canadian Evangelicals was held in Vancouver in February, 1909. Delegates moved that their college follow the precepts of Wycliffe, and Owen suggested it be named for Hugh Latimer, one of the leaders of the Protestant movement in England, chaplain to Henry VIII, and Bishop of Worcester. (He was burned at the stake by Mary I. "Be of good cheer, Master Ridley," said Latimer, as the flames rose. "We shall this day light such a candle. . .as shall never be put out."

Bishop Dart had been injured in a railway accident and much of the diocesan work had been assumed by Archdeacon Pentreath; which explains, suggests one observer, "how he let this end run be made around him." One day, the bishop opened his *Vancouver Province* and learned of the Evangelicals' plan. He was not pleased. "This movement," he told a Kootenay Synod, "I utterly condemn, and my brother Bishop of Columbia entirely agrees with me."

Owen wrote the bishop, insisting that he and his group had "no disloyal feelings toward the Church authorities." He had called at Dart's home, intending to tell him of their plans, but the bishop was not in. The bishop wrote back, pointing out that he had been frequently in Christ Church, where the rector might have approached him, and concluding: "I could not recognize in any way your proposed rival Theological College in my diocese."

Nevertheless, Latimer College was established in 1910, with the Reverend W.H. Vance as principal. Vance, yet another Wycliffe College alumnus, was then rector of the Church of the Ascension, Toronto. His selection was made by Dr. V.N. Hoyles, president of Wycliffe; the Reverend T.R. O'Meara, principal of Wycliffe; the Reverend Dr. H.J. Cody, St. Paul's Church, Toronto; and Owen. It was approved by the Colonial and Continental Church Society, which had demanded participation in the selection of a principal in return for financial assistance.

How John Dart would have responded to the arrival of Vance in Vancouver cannot be known, for the bishop suffered a paralytic stroke on April 6, 1910, and on April 15, he died.

In the fifteen years of John Dart's episcopate, the number of clergy in the diocese (including Kootenay) grew from nineteen to sixty-six; three-quarters of the endowment for the Kootenay bishopric was raised; a fund for widows and orphans and a clergy superannuation fund were established; mission work was begun or extended by the Columbia Coast Mission and Missions to Seamen; permanent Chinese and Japanese missions were funded; St. George's Industrial School for Indians was opened at Lytton; a diocesan branch of the Women's Auxiliary was formed (its motto: *Thy Kingdom come;* its colors: royal blue and gold); the Diocese of New Westminster was divided into rural deaneries (Vancouver, New Westminster and Lytton); and the province began moving, if somewhat disagreeably, toward a theological college.

The diocese was growing. In 1897, a "fey Irishman" named James Burnes had taken his family to North Vancouver for a picnic and decided to stay there. His wife wanted a church, so he set about designing and building St. John's.

In 1901, the Reverend Douglas Davies-Moore preached the first sermon in All Saints', Mission City, to a congregation of

Children of St. Mark's, Kitsilano, about 1909, when the church stood at First and Maple. Services were conducted by Arthur "Sovvy" Sovereign, Christ Church assistant who became Bishop of Yukon and then, six months later, when Renison went to St. Paul's, Toronto, Bishop of Athabasca.

seventy-two – including most of the settlement's citizens. The offertory totaled $4.40.

The Reverend E.M. Searles, a onetime Okanagan bar-keeper, became vicar of Camp Slough, Cheam and East Chilliwack, and the first priest at St. Peter's in Rosedale.

In 1908, services began to be held in a classic little red schoolhouse at Boundary Bay, the nucleus of the future St. David's. "A pump organ was purchased at a cost of $38.00 plus freight of $16.00," noted founder Robert Smith in his diary.

And in 1910, St. Stephen's, Summerland, was built to replace the tiny pioneer church in Giant's Head Road Cemetery. The original church had burned down during a parish clean-up bee.

The Rev. C.C. Croucher, who had been Acton Sillitoe's chaplain, at St. John's Church in Yale —first used as a school by the Ditchingham Sisters. With Croucher are Mrs. Croucher and Mrs. Street.

De Pencier—not merely an heroic figure, but a genuine hero, in his diocese and in battle.

He looked like a soldier, even when he wasn't in his battalion chaplain's uniform or his ribboned and medalled robes. "Tall, well built, of military bearing," said *The Canadian Churchman,* "clear-headed, energetic and business-like." And he used his episcopal authority the way a soldier would. "A forceful person," Hilda Hellaby remembers, "ran his diocese with a stern hand." He was Adam Urias de Pencier, and the Diocese of New Westminster was under his command for three decades.

The first de Pencier in North America was not a de Pencier at all; he was a von Pincer. Christian von Pincer, member of a family whose crest had been registered in Berlin in 1615, was a captain in von Riedesel's dragoons, a regiment of Hessian mercenaries which fought for the British in the American Revolutionary War. After the war, von Pincer settled in Quebec, married a Canadienne, and changed his name to de Pencier. His son Luke joined a company of United Empire Loyalists given crown land in Ontario. In 1866, at Burritt's Rapids, von Pincer's great-grandson, the future Bishop of New Westminster, was born.

Adam de Pencier taught school for several years before his ordination. Then he studied at Trinity College, Toronto, and worked as priest-vicar of the Cathedral Church of St. Alban the Martyr. He was present at the historic General Synod of 1893. That same year, he married Nina Fredericka Wells, daughter of Lieutenant-Colonel Frederick Wells of Toronto.

In 1901, de Pencier was curate of the Cathedral Church of St. James. Three years later he moved west to Brandon, where, from the pulpit of St. Matthew's, his powerful voice reached crowds standing in the street. In 1908, he became rector of St. Paul's, Vancouver, and it was in that West End church on the Feast of St. James, 1910, that the 44-year-old priest became the first Anglican bishop to be consecrated west of the Rockies. The Primate of All Canada, the Most Reverend Samuel Matheson, celebrated Holy Communion, examined the bishop-elect, and said the Prayer for the Church Militant.

A month before, de Pencier had been elected by synod at Holy Trinity Cathedral, New Westminster. The voting had gone through four ballots. The other nominees for the see made vacant by the April death of John Dart were the Venerable Edwyn S.W. Pentreath, Archdeacon of Columbia since 1897, and Canon Norman Tucker, rector of Christ Church in 1894, now first

General Secretary of the Mission Society of the Canadian Church.

"For the first two or three ballots," wrote one observer, "there was a standoff between a very high and a very low churchman, both well-loved and saintly men, but each repugnant to the other's party."

Archdeacon Pentreath, who had served Bishop Dart as "the architect of the diocese," and Canon Tucker, who was nominated by the rebellious Christ Church rector, C.C. Owen, might have been regarded as the respective choices of the diocese's Anglo-Catholic and Evangelical factions; but, in fact, the contest was between Pentreath and de Pencier. Tucker was never in the lead in balloting by either clerical or lay delegates. (He never received more than five of the thirty-six clerical votes and on the last two ballots got none. Where was Owen?) De Pencier led all the clerical votes; Pentreath led the lay voting on the first two ballots.

On the fourth ballot, there was a final shift of lay votes to de Pencier, and Pentreath—who was chairman of synod—declared the West End rector bishop and promised loyalty to his office.

The de Penciers at home: Nina and Adam with children Eric, Joseph and Theo (rear), Adam, Betty, Nina and John (front). John died in WW I, Adam in WW II. Theo became one of the diocese's most loved priests.

Latimer Hall students and staff, 1912-13. Rear: F.M.D. Ryan, Lim Yuen, F. Wilkinson, E. Buli, K.B Framptong, O.C. Esperson. Front: A.H. Sovereign, G.H. Wilson, Dr. W.H. Vance, C.C. Owen.

One of the new bishop's first problems was the proposed theological college – or colleges. W.H. Vance had arrived in Vancouver to be principal of Bishop Latimer College and the school was opened in a house on Haro Street, in the city's West End, in October, 1910. A.H. "Sovvy" Sovereign was made lecturer in dogmatics, and soon the Reverend H.R. Trumpour and the Reverend H.G. Miller were added to the teaching staff. Even so, the supporters of St. Mark's were not prepared to give up their college, and in 1912 it opened on Davie Street, a five-minute stroll from Haro. The principal was the Reverend C.A. Seager, formerly of Vernon, but more recently rector of St. Cyprian's, Toronto. Seager had given the sermon at de Pencier's consecration. (Later he became provost of Trinity College and, ultimately, Bishop of Ontario.)

K.B. Frampton was a member of the first class in the house on Haro. "It was the custom of Cecil Owen," wrote Frampton, "to invite to the Vicarage for refreshments after Evensong any young people in the congregation who were away from home. It was on one of these occasions that he dropped the bait to me...."We were a happy crowd at Latimer, and most of us joined into the life of Western McGill, which became UBC. Rugger was my game....“Bertie Wardle was the one that gave us our headaches. He once, when out with some of the boys to Capilano, climbed over the side rope of the suspension bridge, under the footway, and then up over the other side....“Although most of my ministry had been spent in England, I am always grateful for the training I received at Latimer, and for its quiet devotional life. We were always on good terms with St. Mark’s and prayed for the day when these two Halls would be one.”

Norman Larmonth, who later became famous as the diocese’s most effective fund raiser, was one of the first dozen students at St. Mark’s. Only one, he noted, was Canadian. The others came from England, Scotland, Ireland and Japan. “Everything was primitive at 1249 Davie...there was only one room to serve as chapel, lecture room and common room...the only window looked up to heaven. Dr. Seager had two ideals for his College. First, there was to be only one rule, and this was a moral sense of responsibility....the other ideal was for each one of us to give the first five years of our Priesthood to the Church as celibates; if we did, the Bishops could send us wherever the need was greatest....but humour was part of our lives as well...an elderly Priest gave us the following advice: ‘During the first two years of my Ministry, I wrote some ninety-two sermons, and with a little revision they have done me ever since.’”

While the two colleges were blocks apart physically and miles apart philosophically, their eventual union was determined on November 29, 1910, when British Columbia’s three bishops – Perrin of Columbia, Du Vernet of Caledonia (who had taught at Wycliffe) and de Pencier of New Westminster and Kootenay – presented their “Plan for Theological Education in the Church of England in the Province of British Columbia.”

The plan called for the formation of an Anglican Theological College (ATC) to oversee the work of both Bishop Latimer and St. Mark’s Colleges. The board of governors of ATC would include the bishops of the British Columbia dioceses, three lay and three clerical delegates from each diocese, and the heads of St. Mark’s and Bishop Latimer (*ex officio*). The two colleges (or “halls”) would erect their own buildings, hire their own staff and collect their own funds, but students would be registered in the Anglican Theological College and that institution would issue all diplomas. Furthermore, ATC would control the theological education funds of the dioceses and would represent the church in all dealings with the government, specifically in negotiations involving the University of British Columbia. The site allotted to the church by the university would be divided into four parts, one each for St. Mark’s and Bishop Latimer, two for common purposes.

The rival colleges were not brought together at UBC until 1927, but common lectures were given as early as 1914. The bishops’ bold move of 1910 had provided the matrix for the training of Anglican priests in British Columbia.

"As it was summer," wrote Mrs. Herbert Beeman, "we erected a large tent with a wooden floor and sides on the land we soon acquired." Mrs. Beeman was one of the founders of St. Mary's, Kerrisdale. The first congregation (12) met in a schoolroom, sat at children's desks and passed a candy box to take collection. When the candy box had been sufficiently sweetened, they bought the land on Whitehead Road.

"I was elected organist," continued Mrs. Beeman. "I had always been 'allergic' to spiders and those summer mornings I realized the truth of the theory that spiders like music. As I sat at the organ, pedaling hard, to my horror I saw the long-legged garden variety running in my direction. I tried to pedal with one foot and kick out the spiders with the other! As I was in full view of the congregation, I knew they wondered what on earth was the matter with me.

"At last the day came, in 1913, when the cornerstone was laid for our real church building. Then we accumulated 12 little choir boys. We also had a fine choir outside the church – hundreds of little frogs croaking in the pools between the stumps. . .their voices were strong and hearty.

"One night I noticed a lot of giggling among the boys and, looking down the chancel, I saw the reason. A dozen or so of the little frogs were hopping about, brought in a box by a very angelic-looking little boy.

"Our organ was one of the kind having dummy pipes (so impressive!). It had to be blown by hand and we were lucky enough to have, believe it or not, two boys whose surname was Blow. They kindly obliged by filling the organ with the necessary wind..."

In the parish of St. Nicolas, in what was called East Vancouver Heights, the Reverend D. Davies-Moore complained, "There are a number of beautiful residences, but unfortunately for us it has happened that all of the wealthy families are Scotch Presbyterians."

Mr. Davies-Moore continued, "Many monied English Church people arrive here bringing with them pronounced Socialistic ideas of a nature antagonizing to the old Church. Most of them devote the whole of Sunday to house-building and gardening, and altogether set a dreadful example to the Canadian residents. Very few of them have ever come even once to our services, and they will do nothing at all to assist in the heavy financial burdens created to provide here a place of worship."

But, he concluded, "They will learn that we really love them and are not simply after their money, as many now say we are. They will, in time, learn to do their share in meeting financial responsibilities, and come to love the English Church of Canada."

In 1912, West Vancouver seceded from North Vancouver and became a municipality of its own. Anglican families there began the Dundarave Mission in Mr. E. Wyatt's camp. Students from St. Mark's came across Burrard Inlet to conduct services, receiving for travel expenses one dollar per month. The mission became the parish of St. Stephen's.

Arthur Sovereign had become rector of St. Mark's, Kitsilano, and he asked his Latimer College colleague, H.R. Trumpour, to oversee the Point Grey Missionary District – the beginnings of St. Helen's. Early services were held in a school, and the first large congregation was truly a captive audience: thirty inmates of the Boys' Reformatory. The following Sunday, Mr. Trumpour found a note from the schoolteacher asking him to request his congregation to refrain from carrying away the contents of the desks.

In those same pre-war years, another St.

Helen's was being built, in South Westminster. "Everyone thought," wrote W.W. Hastings, "that the area was destined to become the metropolis of the Fraser Valley.

"Because religious worship was a part of community life, churches also served as gathering places where everybody met everybody else and news and gossip were exchanged. Realizing this, a wealthy real estate developer, W.J. Walker, decided to build a church suitable for a burgeoning area and bought some land on Old Yale Road at the top of the hill. . . .Perhaps because of nostalgia for the ancient churches of his native England. . .he decided to build a replica of an old English church. . . ."

The metropolis never came, but the stately church has remained one of the most charming in the diocese. It was designed by Frank W. Macey and built of native fir. The main tower was sheathed in copper and contained a revolving beacon light. The altars are of cypress from the Mount of Olives, the chimes are from England. And the central stained glass panel in the east window is now a memorial to Walker, onetime reeve of Surrey and the provider of two other churches: St. Oswald's, Port Kells, and St. Aidan's, Tynehead.

The Rev. and Mrs. W.H.G. Battershill in their Sea Island cottage, rented from Jacob Grauer. In 1911, Battershill had charge of both St. Augustine's, Marpole, and St. Mary's, Kerrisdale.

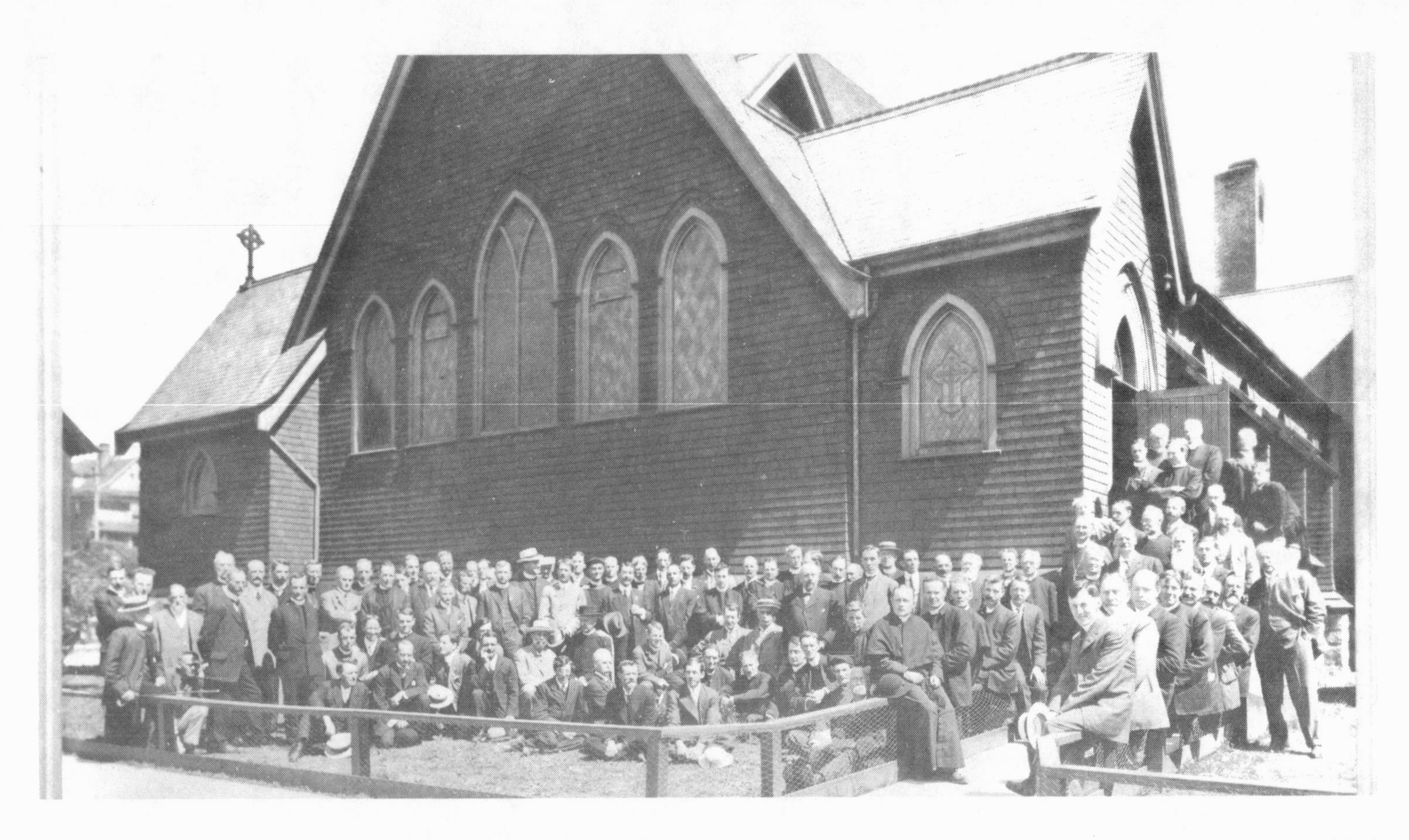

Diocesan Synod, 1912. The Diocese of New Westminster still administered the Diocese of Kootenay (and would until 1915) and the area that would become the Diocese of Cariboo (to remain under Bishop —later Archbishop—de Pencier until it elected its first bishop in 1925).

In Vancouver, Bishop de Pencier consecrated the chancel of the new parish church of St. Mary the Virgin, South Hill, built as a memorial to Bishop George Hills.

And where Burnaby meets New Westminster, Victor Wright was going to St. Alban's, "a little brown church hidden behind a dense stand of fir trees that bordered what was then Douglas Road.

"The church was much smaller and darker, because of the trees all around it. It was quieter, too, for traffic, especially on Sundays, was very much lighter. There was no need of a loudspeaker system, for the occasional hum of a passing motor hardly stirred the quiet order of the service, accompanied by a rather asthmatic harmonium.

"One of my fondest memories is being taken as a child to Evensong by my parents. We would walk to the church, and sing the well-known hymns, and hear the cadences of the Prayer Book and the Bible. Then, the lights would be turned out, except for the one over the pulpit, and Mr. Thompson, then the rector, would preach.

"The church was not impressive, it was humble. What came most clearly to me was the warmth and security, something that a child always needs, a blessing given to me and to many others on those quiet Sundays that seem so long ago."

In 1910, St. James's celebrated the twenty-fifth anniversary of Father Clinton's arrival to be rector of Granville. Among the hundreds of guests were many of the builders of Vancouver – Richard Alexander, Harry Abbott, H.J. Cambie, S. Garvin, William McGeer, Campbell Sweeney, Thomas Evans, Dr. Bell-Irving, Captain Soule. Two years later, an even larger crowd lined the streets of the city as the pioneer priest's funeral cortege moved toward Mountain View Cemetery. Bishop de Pencier conducted a Solemn Requiem Mass, including a hymn Father Clinton had written originally in Swahili for the Christians of Zanzibar.

Captain John Antle of the Columbia Coast Mission had another boat, the 100-foot *Columbia II*. "A doctor was on board," writes Marion Antle Mennes, "and a surgery with an X-ray machine, and cupboards filled with all sorts of medications, bandages, splints and plaster of Paris, enough to fill any doctor's heart with pleasure. An operating table and two hospital beds were nailed down to the floor in case of rough weather."

Columbia II put in wherever the emer-

The CCM hospital ship *Columbia* makes a house call on a floating home in Retreat Pass.

Sunday school teachers at St. Mark's, Kitsilano, in 1912—the sunny days before the war. "Sovvy" Sovereign (centre) was also responsible for the Point Grey Missionary District.

gency white flag waved. But it was also, says the captain's daughter, "a delight for the fast-growing Antle family on their summer holidays. . . .

"On a long journey. . .Father, in the pilot house, got bored with looking at a vast expanse of grayish sea and sent for me to relieve him. 'Now,' he'd say, 'get up on the high stool and keep her nose on that mark on the compass. If you see another boat coming, ring the bell and I'll come up.' Then he'd disappear down into the saloon and stretch out on the locker behind the stove and read." The substitute skipper was not yet old enough to read.

A constitution for the Ecclesiastical Province of British Columbia had been drafted in 1910; it was put into effect at the first provincial synod, held in Victoria on February 18, 1914. Frederick Du Vernet, Bishop of Caledonia, was elected Metropolitan.

The 1913 caption on this photograph identifies the seven men as Columbia Coast Mission "Sky Pilots" from the Diocese of New Westminster. The squadron lined up and grinned for the camera in Yellowhead Pass in the Rocky Mountains—once a route to the Cariboo gold fields.

The first Provincial Synod of British Columbia met in 1914 in Victoria. Bishop Frederick Du Vernet (centre front) of Caledonia was elected Metropolitan. Bishop de Pencier is at his right; C.A. Seager of St. Mark's, later Metropolitan of Ontario, stands directly behind Bishop de Pencier.

The Diocese of Kootenay became independent of New Westminster that same year with the election of a bishop for the mountain country: Alexander John Doull, Dean of Christ Church Cathedral, Victoria. Now it was time for Cariboo to become a diocese, and New Westminster Synod approved that resolution. Cariboo, however, was to remain under Bishop de Pencier's administration until 1925.

For the next four years, that administration would be directed by the Venerable Francis Heathcote, who had come from Winnipeg to be Archdeacon of Columbia after the death of Edwyn Pentreath in 1913. War had broken out in Europe, and Adam de Pencier changed his purple for khaki.

As an honorary captain in the Canadian Chaplain Services, the bishop was attached to the 62nd Overseas Battalion, Canadian Expeditionary Forces. He served in France and Belgium and was twice mentioned in despatches. He worked at hospitals and casualty depots, and travelled between Popringe and the Swiss border, administering confirmation to the men in the lines.

At Christ Church, Vancouver, Cecil Owen received a letter from his only son, Harold. The letter, says Hilda Hellaby, "said how much men over there needed consolation and strength and what a lot of work a chaplain could do." The next message from Europe said that Harold had been killed. Owen left his pulpit and went to Europe.

Edith Powis remembers the April day when St. Mark's was built in Kitsilano: "We made a congregational picnic of it. The men took their tools and the W.A. made up all sorts of foods. There were my eldest brother, Sidney Cunliffe, and the Atcheson boys, the Haymer boys, the Jones boys, the Dawe boys. Just seems as though it happened yesterday." But not long after the church-raising picnic, "quite a number of our boys were wiped out at Vimy Ridge. . . ."

When the war ended, Major Cecil Owen returned to Vancouver and became chaplain of Vancouver General Hospital. Lieutenant-Colonel de Pencier was summoned to Buckingham Palace and invested in the Order of the British Empire by King George V.

C.C. Owen, pied piper of the priesthood. *Canadian Churchman* called him "manly, fearless."

"Two of our babies, sent from China," wrote Hilda Hellaby on this 1925 Vancouver snapshot.

"With a population pouring in from all quarters of the globe," declared Bishop de Pencier in New Westminster, "the efforts that are necessary so that the church. . . may give her due proportion of influence to the moulding and shaping of these growing communities. . .should be measured by our utmost ability.

"The call to each of us. . .is definite and clear: that as Christians we so live and work that we make it easier for others to become Christians too."

In 1914, the Reverend Francis Cassilis Kennedy had come to Vancouver, after two decades in Japan, to be superintendent of Japanese Missions. "A very nice man," says Hilda Hellaby. "I think he had been greatly influenced by his work among the Japanese; he had the same sort of manner." (At the same time, he was "typically Torontonian." Ah, the mysterious East.)

Three years later, the Reverend Neville Lascelles Ward came from Honan to be superintendent of Chinese Missions. One of his workers was Hilda Hellaby, whom he taught the Cantonese dialect. Ward was, she remembers, "very eccentric. And very clever. At that time, nobody wore beards except a few eccentric old gentlemen, but he did, and it was red."

Captain Cornelius Porter of the Church Army led the diocese's East Indian Mission at All Saints'. Porter worked among Mohammedans, Hindus and Sikhs, teaching them first English and then the Gospel. He was, said All Saints rector Lewis Hooper, "a man full of the Holy Ghost and of faith. . . .a street preacher of force, and a quiet worker among. . .men and women the Church does not usually reach." But when the mission was only two years old, Porter died, and the diocese's work among East Indians ended.

Ward moved on to the United States in 1926 and Kennedy became superintendent of both Japanese and Chinese missions. Kennedy, the longtime Matsumoto missionary, was not well, but he worked hard to bring accord between Asiatics and Occidentals. Besides doing his mission work, he wrote, lectured, and represented Canada at Pan-Pacific Conferences in Hawaii and Kyoto. "His efforts against racial discrimination and his good work for the Japanese were so vigorous," wrote Timothy Nakayama, "that he was accused by some of receiving money from the Japanese government. . . ." In fact, it was the Japanese community of Vancouver which raised money for Kennedy's care and the support of his family when the priest had lung surgery.

In 1930, Kennedy was taken to St. Paul's Hospital, seriously ill. He said, "I must go to North Vancouver to speak about the Japanese problem," and died. His funeral service was conducted in Japanese, Chinese and English.

Hilda Hellaby organized a Church Boys' League in the Chinese community ("those fellows are now middle-aged men with grown-up children") and adopted a Chinese baby. She named her daughter Felicity.

Missions to the Orientals, says Dr. Hellaby, were "always a rather unpopular piece of work; those of us who worked among them came in for a bit of hostility." The church believed it had a duty to evangelize among Orientals, but it was not convinced of an equality between races. "There wasn't the feeling that we are all brothers and sisters in Christ."

First graduates of Anglican Theological College after St. Mark's and Latimer were united. ATC was, says Hilda Hellaby, "our first introduction to any deep philosophical view."

H.J. Cambie, a founder of Christ Church, daughter and son-in-law, the Rev. and Mrs. C.S. McGaffin.

This cartoon by the Reverend E.O. Robathan illustrates the cheerful compromise worked out between the St. Mark's "Anglo-Catholics" and the Latimer Hall "Evangelicals" at UBC's ATC.

In 1927, the Governor-General of Canada, Lord Willingdon, performed the ritual sod-turning for the Anglican Theological College at the University of British Columbia (then a modest assembly of army barracks). The college was formally opened by the Primate, Archbishop Matheson. It was, wrote Mary Doris Burton in *Unity in Diversity*, "a step in faith, an adventure into the unknown. [ATC] stood in stark contrast to Wycliffe and Trinity Colleges, which continued to exist separately, across the street from each other, professing to be part of the same faith, yet unable to work together in it. The British Columbian church, in an independent fashion quite typical of the province in which it was situated, had worked out an innovative solution for the handling of religious partisanship within theological education. With this, it challenged the rest of the Anglican Church."

Lord Willingdon turned the sod for ATC. Left to right: Archbishop de Pencier, Bishop Schofield (B.C.), the Governor General, Mrs. W.H. Vance, Lady Willingdon, Dr. Vance, Bishop Doull (Kootenay).

Boy Scouts and Cubs, Girl Guides and Brownies, attached to St. Paul's, Powell River—a 1920 version of a perennial parish activity.

After World War I, the B.C. forest industry was booming, and many Old Country families, veterans and war brides moved to Powell River.

Adam de Pencier became Metropolitan of British Columbia in 1925. One of his first acts was the consecration, on Michaelmas Day, of the splendid Walter Robert Adams as Bishop of Cariboo.

Four years later, as the diocese celebrated its Golden Jubilee (Lord and Lady Willingdon were guests at the Jubilee banquet), Archbishop de Pencier announced the selection of Christ Church as his cathedral. The Vancouver church would be required to replace the Holy Table collection plate with a cross. No longer would it be known as "St. Alms' Dish."

Christ Church rector Robert J. Renison became the first Dean of the Cathedral. Renison had been born in Tipperary, educated at Wycliffe. He enlisted in the Boer War as "Patrick O'Reilly". Returning to Canada, he worked fourteen years as a missionary among the Indians of Moosonee. Later he wrote a regular column for the *Toronto Globe & Mail.* (A devoted reader was Vancouver Police Chief Walter Mulligan, a central figure in the famous "police probe" of the 1950s. Mulligan had two years of Renison's columns carefully saved.)

There had been episcopal rumblings about changing the see to Vancouver since 1898. Now the time had come. (Christ Church was not de Pencier's first choice. There had been plans to build a see house and cathedral on South Granville, where St. John's, Shaughnessy, now stands. Pledge cards were printed in an attempt to raise funds for a new cathedral there.)

The people of Holy Trinity in New Westminster were not amused—"bitterly disappointed" is Leslie Pearson's description—and, according to Harry Ratcliff, "New Westminster city council was furious when word reached it. . .I understand they made the bishop a prisoner in his own See House on Agnes Street until they came to terms."

The terms included Holy Trinity's right to retain the title "Cathedral" and to receive half the revenue from the sale of the New Westminster see house property. Agreement was reached in time to prevent civil court action and the playing out in Supreme Court of a Trollopean church comedy.

Robert J. Renison, missionary to the Moosonee Indians, first dean of Christ Church Cathedral.

Opposite: Pledge card. *Above:* Holy Trinity Cathedral Choir, 1920. *Rear:* H. Hill, R. Dingle, B. Sharpe, C. Silva-White, D. Jennings (organist), V. Herring, Canon d'Easum, Mr. Oates, A. Beatty, C. Littlewood. Women: Mrs. Broad, Miss Jones, Mrs. Payne, Mrs. Elsom, Miss W. Turnball, Mrs. Mahoney, Mrs.

ORIGINAL

Cathedral and See House Site Fund

Amount required *now* $3,750.00 to take up the option on site.
Amount required in Six Months $3,750.00, plus Interest.

I promise to pay $.. to the Bishop of New Westminster, for purchase of Site, corner of Granville Street and 26th Avenue, for the new See House and Cathedral.

1st Payment............................*$*............ *2nd Payment*............................*$*............

Name..

....

The Site contains 3 1-10 acres. The terms of payment are spread over ten years. The Executive Committee approves of the Option being taken up, on condition that the First Two Payments are provided for.

(*Cont.*) Woods, Miss E. D'Easum, Mrs. Herring, Mrs. Littlewood, Mrs. B. Sharpe, Miss Appleton, Mrs. Shuttleworth, unidentified. Sides: Mr. Whetmore, Mr. Shuttleworth. Boys: J. d'Easum (organ pumper), G. Dingle, Mr. Dalgleish, T. Whetmore, G. Charles, B. Dingle, G. Heaps, H. Dawe, H. Hill, F. Nelson.

Early Columbia Coast Mission hospital staff: Dr. Daril P. Hannington and Nurses Sutherland and Franklin. CCM built four hospitals between Georgia Strait and Queen Charlotte Sound.

Archbishop de Pencier's son Theo was posted to Lytton, then given charge of the old church of St. John the Divine, built at Derby by the Royal Engineers in 1859 and later floated across the river to Maple Ridge. In the Caulfeild district of West Vancouver, church services were held in private homes. By 1927, St. Francis-in-the-Wood was built.

Church activities were community events. Reeve Thomas Brooks of South Vancouver opened a "Pedlar's Fair" in the Horticultural Hall at St. Mary's. "Madame X" told fortunes, and the congregation and friends were asked to "please keep in mind the dates of the entertainment *Browne with an E* and songs from *Geisha* and *San Toy* by members of the Building Committee and Choir."

In Mission, the Reverend Heber Greene began camp services for berry pickers on the King-Beach and Shook fruit farms.

At St. Alban's in Richmond, the dramatic club became known for its production of plays like *The Monkey's Paw.* "St. Alban's Parish was the cultural centre of the community," wrote Betty Ball. "The Lulu Island Parish Picnic was something to remember. A double-header inter-urban tram. . . bedecked with a large banner. . .would pick up a happy crowd. . .and proceed to [Stanley] Park." Rector of St. Alban's in 1930 was the Reverend A.J. Williams. Mrs. Williams, a nurse, dispensed medical advice to the community (there was no resident medical authority on the island) and, on Sundays, "was also a very good soprano for the choir." The four Williams children "also gave great assistance, not to mention Grandpa, Mrs. Williams' father. On Sunday, Grandpa Howland, a very distinguished looking gentleman with white hair and beard, was a valuable tenor. . .on weekdays [he] was the janitor."

"Everything was ready, even the usual stiff southeaster," wrote John Antle. It was Christmas, 1929, aboard the *Columbia.* "Away we went for Echo Bay, a floating village. . . .In the *Columbia*'s cabin. . .a gaily decorated tree, properly secured for stormy weather, sparkled forth its welcome. Soon the ringing of the ship's bell and the tooting of the whistle announced the approach of Santa, with his bags filled with presents, not only for the kids but for grown people also. . . .Dr. Stringer's hospital looked more like the toy department in Timothy Eaton's . . . .Cecil Fitzgerald, the *Columbia*'s engineer, had assumed his usual role of Santa Claus...."

That year, Antle's Columbia Coast Mission built St. Mary's Hospital at Pender Harbor. And work continued at Kingcome Inlet Mission, the Indian village Margaret Craven wrote of later in *I Heard the Owl Call My Name.* When the Columbia Coast Mission built a school at Kingcome, three bands of the Kwakiutl tribe lived there, fishing for oolichan and salmon. The Reverend W. Govier baptized the village chief, but much of the Kingcome mission work was done by deaconesses. Two were Margaret Solomon, a nurse, and Edith Adams, a teacher, who were ordered deaconesses at Christ Church in 1931. "We were really going to live at Kingcome Indian Reserve all winter," they wrote breathlessly in the *Log of the Columbia.* "Kingcome is one of Nature's beauty spots. The river winds in and out the valleys between the mountains until Kingcome Indian Reserve is encircled by mountains...."

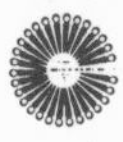

St. George's Church, Kingcome Inlet. The totem pole is a memorial to King George V.

Father Harold Whitehead, Miss Phyllis Cooper and Father Wilberforce Cooper at St. James's Clergy House. They had come to "see what was happening on the other side of the Rocky Mountains."

In the oldest part of Vancouver, a trio of priests became the first residents of the St. James's clergy house. They were Wilberforce Cooper, a London slum worker, schooled at Keble College, who had come to the Cariboo, with his sister Phyllis, after service as an army chaplain; Harold Whitehead, another Londoner, most recently in Florence; and Bruce Reddish, an Ohioan who had been working in New York. When Father Reddish moved on to Puerto Rico, his place was taken by Eric Munn (later Bishop of Caledonia), who taught Greek to the girls at St. Marina's School.

"The head of the morality squad at the police station was a good friend," wrote Father Cooper. "He once told the Order of St. Michael that we had 85 per cent of the major crime of Greater Vancouver domiciled in our parish. That," said Father Cooper cheerfully, "no doubt was true."

Father Cooper was known as "the best touch on skid road." "They don't all get gospel who knock on the paneled vestry door," wrote the *Vancouver Province.* "If they're hungry, they get. . .coffee and pie, or a meal. There's generally a pair of shoes around if somebody needs them...." One day Father Cooper gave away a pair that belonged to the visiting brother of one of the other priests. "Doesn't do to leave anything lying around," said Wilberforce Cooper.

Father Whitehead had a fine acerbic wit. Once, as rural dean, he was required to take part in a certain parish's deliberations on the engaging of a new priest. The meeting dragged on for hours, with the parish committee never getting near agreement. Finally, Father Whitehead adjourned the meeting with a prayer: "Oh God," he solemnly intoned, "send these people the succour they need."

The St. James's clergy heard a lot of knocks on their Cordova Street door during the Great Depression of the 1930s. "All the East End churches got involved in relief work," said Hilda Hellaby, "because the government hadn't been prepared for the Depression. At one time we were feeding a thousand men a day."

"We slept men in the two rooms below the Bishop's Room," said Father Cooper. "I remember putting a notice on the alms box, 'Kind Burglar: Please don't spoil the box; it's emptied every day.'"

"Spencer's provided us with mattresses," says Father Bill Youngman, then a St. James's layman, "Hudson's Bay with blankets, and Woodward's, who were good members of St. James's, sent all the day-old bread plus peanut butter and other things to keep the bread line going. Occasionally there'd be some tobacco and cigarette papers to help the men along the road."

"We held a regular outdoor mission," wrote Father Cooper. "One of our first missions was to Hogan's Alley, a notorious spot towards the south end of Gore Avenue. Miss Cooper [played] the harmonium."

"One night," remembers Bill Youngman, "a stranger started to heckle Father Cooper during his address. This didn't suit the usual crowd of skid road folks. Some of them got up, grabbed the heckler, took him down on the tracks between the warehouses, beat the daylights out of him, came back, sat on the sidewalk and took out of their pockets a little bottle and had a nip – anything from canned heat to hair tonic. And one remarked, 'He can't do that, because that's our pal standing there.'"

"The best touch on skid road"—Father Cooper. The ex-London slum worker spent 39 years here.

Opening night at the Missions to Seamen Hall in 1923, 26 years after Father Clinton started the waterfront mission next to St. James's. The new hall was in Dr. Henry Bell-Irving's old home on Hastings Street. The Flying Angel symbol is on the banner beside the enormous Union Jack.

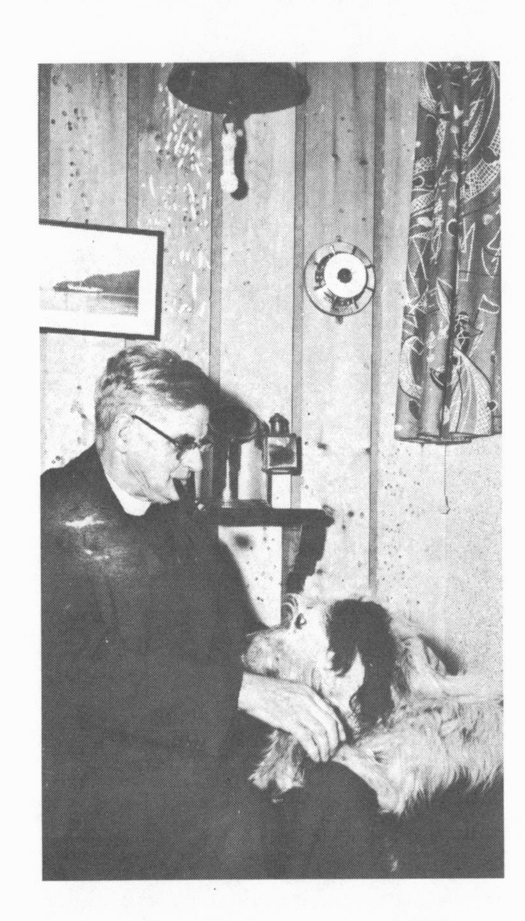

W.J. Leighton, seamen's chaplain 1935-1954. Seamen still talk about "the padre and his dog."

Bishop Winnington Ingram at Lambeth Pier, London, 1933, dedicates motor yacht *John Antle*.

Dr. W.T. Lockhart, ship's surgeon on the *Columbia*, helps a young patient back to land.

Archbishop Scott, Primate, moderator of the Central Committee of the World Council of Churches.

Ted Scott (second from right), in 1929, when his father was rector of All Saints', Ladner.

A Holy Trinity Church history says, "The Depression changed the moral outlook of Canadians, and nowhere more than in Vancouver. There was a new social consciousness." An acute observer of these changes was the teenage son of the rector of St. Nicolas's, in the East Vancouver-North Burnaby area. The rector was Tom Walter Scott. The son, Ted, would become, forty years later, Primate of All Canada.

"In the parish that Dad was in," says Ted Scott, "about 64 per cent of the families were on relief. It was in the low income area. And that left its mark on me very much. Many other parts of Vancouver where you didn't have that same level of unemployment seemed to have minimum concern about what was happening to those people. It was that kind of thing that bothered me, the way that cities become ghetto-ized. One part doesn't really know what's happening in the other, and there isn't that much deep concern, or didn't seem to be; and I know a lot of the boys at college [ATC] got quite a good eye-opener when at Christmas I got them to come and help deliver hampers in the parish. They saw a pattern of life they had never known existed in this area.

"The thirties were pretty rough times and

The congregation of the old St. Mark's, Second at Larch, Kitsilano —one of the three Diocese of New Westminster parishes where Canon Tom Scott served as priest. This snapshot, remembers his daughter, Dorothy Sullivan, was taken at "a painting bee we held to paint the church."

Young unemployed men march through the streets of Vancouver in the Hungry Thirties.

Canoers at Artaban, begun as a camp mission in 1923, at Long Bay on Gambier Island.

there were some quite strong tensions in the life of the church about how it should be responding to those kinds of issues.

"There wasn't enough concern. . .about what was happening to people in the structures of society. One of my most vivid memories. . .is going down to the Post Office during the sit-down strike of the unemployed in Vancouver. . .and finding two boys I'd gone to school with in Caron, Saskatchewan. There hadn't been a crop around Caron in six and a half years. There was nothing for them around Vancouver, but if they went back to Caron, it was going back to stagnate....

"There seemed to be no on-going policy and the church didn't seem to be raising that kind of question—and it's always been a problem to me how you can talk about loving your neighbor, loving people, without being concerned about the kind of impact that the conditions they live under have upon them.

"If you really are going to have love and concern for your neighbor, you have to be concerned about legislation and government policies. . .because they affect the lives of people very deeply. One of my memories as a child in Saskatchewan was when a farmer's barn burned down and. . .everybody joined in building a new barn for the farmer.

You had a direct *personal response.* But if you're concerned about housing for somebody in the middle of Vancouver, you can't act that way; you've got to be concerned about the kind of legislation that looks after housing."

Ted Scott worked in four parishes while at college: St. Luke's, St. Augustine's, St. Philip's and Christ Church Cathedral (where he was criticized for "wearing a blue shirt underneath my cassock instead of a white one"). Summers, he worked in the kitchen at Camp Artaban, the Gambier Island camp founded in 1923. When he graduated from ATC, he was ordained to the Bishop of Caledonia and went to work on the Columbia Coast Mission boat running between Kitkatlan and the Alaska Panhandle. He met his wife in one of the villages where the boat docked. Eventually he went to the Winnipeg inner city parish of St. Jude's—named, appropriately, for the patron saint of lost causes.

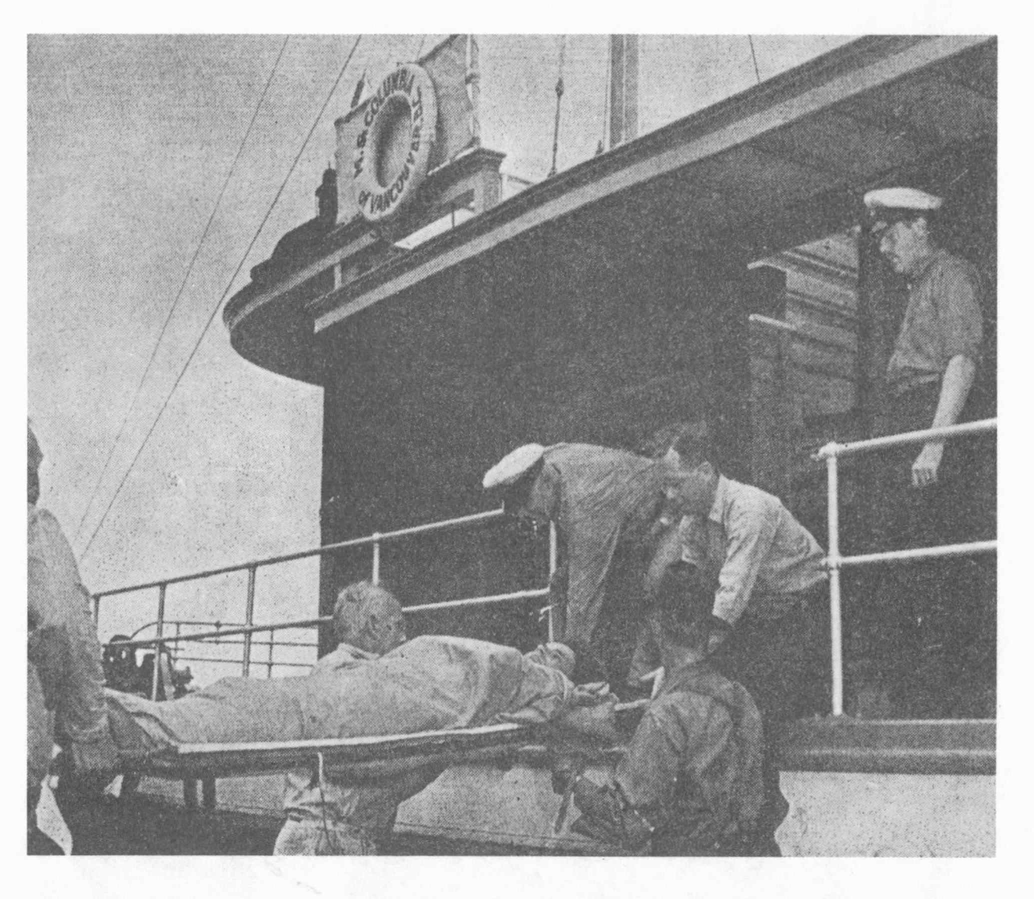

Injured logger is taken on board the *Columbia*. On deck: Captain MacDonald, engineer Bob McCrea and deckhand Bill Durrant. Before Antle's CCM, many loggers were hundreds of miles from hospitals.

Canon Heber Greene of the Columbia Coast Mission baptizing children in the ship's chapel.

ST. MARY'S ANNUAL

PARISH BAZAAR

Wednesday, October 18th, 1922

in St. Mary's Hall

Corner 52nd Avenue and Prince Albert Street

will be opened at 2:30 p.m. by

Mrs. Sillitoe of Vancouver

PARISH GUILD SEWING STALL
Mrs. Fitch (convener); Mrs. Frewin, Mrs. Boxall, Mrs. Walton.

W. A. MISCELLANEOUS STALL, Mrs. Yates (Convener)
Mrs. Yates-Davis, Mrs. Cowling, Mrs. Messenger, Mrs. Mill.

PARISH GUILD FANCY WORK STALL
Miss Hilbert, (convener); Mrs. Marr, Mrs. Bucknall, Mrs. Moxon, Mrs McMurtrie.

GIRLS' W. A. BABY WEAR STALL
Mrs. Jacquot (convener); Miss Hamilton, Miss Rant, Miss Frewin, Miss Thornley.

HOME COOKING STALL
Mrs. Singleton (convener); Mrs. Barraclough, Mrs. Money, Mrs. Wilmot.

SPIDERS WEB—Mrs. Thornley (convener).

REFRESHMENT STALL
Mrs. Guy. (convener); Mrs. C. Cummings, Mrs. Morton, Mrs. A. Cummings.

AFTERNOON TEA, 15 cents, served from 3:30 to 5:00 p.m.

MEAT SUPPER, 35 cents, served from 6 o'clock.

Articles for any of these stalls may be sent to any of the above ladies.
Striping of the Spider's Web at 10:00 p.m.

There will be an INFORMAL CONCERT during the evening
Director: Rev. Jas. MacDougall.

Admission to Bazaar, 10 cents.

Citizen Presses.

For 45 years, Violet Sillitoe was the first lady of the diocese, in demand at parish events.

Violet Sillitoe had remained a celebrity in the diocese. In 1922 St. Mary's, South Hill, advertised its church bazaar with a handbill which announced, in enormous black letters, that the event would be opened by "Mrs. Sillitoe of Vancouver." She attended St. James's, always sitting in the first pew, and she was president of the parish branch of the Woman's Auxiliary. Hilda Hellaby remembers her as "small—and I think she had been quite pretty—and very authoritarian. She was The Bishop's Wife. We all stood rather in awe of her."

But this was the same woman who had been the bride of the handsome minister in Darmstadt, who had sung duets with Princess Louise and solos on the Barkerville stage, who had crawled down the mine shaft at Jack o' Clubs Creek and saddled the horses when the men weren't around; this was the woman who, stepping into a canoe, smiled to hear an Indian guide say, *"Hyas cumtax"* ("She very much understands").

"Dear Violet Sillitoe," said Father Cooper, "when she lay a-dying in 1934, it seemed she had had to make so many speeches in life that she couldn't stop. She said, 'I'm sorry, but the cork's come out; I can't stop.'"

The old St. James's was about to be torn down, to be replaced by the building at Cordova and Gore. Canon A.E. Thain of St. Bartholomew's, Gibson's, asked what would be done with a small rooftop cross. "First come, first served," he was told. So Canon Thain propped a ladder against the church, scaled the roof, and carried the cross away. It still stands atop St. Bartholomew's. Canon Thain also helped build St. Aidan's at Roberts Creek, furnishing it with an altar from St. James's and a bell from Union Steamships.

In 1939, John Antle was retired from the Columbia Coast Mission, but not from the sea. He sailed the 40-foot yawl *Reverie* under (or over) the noses of German submarines on a 347-day voyage from Falmouth to San Diego. "I figured the U-boats wouldn't waste a torpedo on a yawl," said the 75-year-old sailor.

May 14, 1939: The *London Daily Sketch* reported that RAF pilot Adam Eastham de Pencier had "crashed in flames into the sea" by Chesil Beach near Weymouth, a notorious "hoodoo" spot. The archbishop's son was 22.

Archbishop de Pencier announced in 1940 that he would retire. His episcopate had lasted thirty years, and he had honors to last a lifetime. He had been present at the coronations of George V and George VI, he had preached to the King at Westminster Abbey and to the lords and statesmen at the Mansion House, and he had dedicated a totem pole at Kingcome Inlet. The old soldier said, "I am retiring only because I feel that, in justice to the work of the diocese, I should allow a younger and more vigorous successor to take my place." The archbishop was 74. His younger and more vigorous successor was 72.

Violet Sillitoe in the 1930s—half a century after she'd met the dashing chaplain at Darmstadt.

"He loved to play the grand old man," says David Somerville. "And he did it very well."

The Venerable Sir Francis Cooke Caulfeild Heathcote, D.D., Archdeacon of Vancouver and Ninth Baronet of Hursley, was elected Lord Bishop of New Westminster December 10, 1940, at Christ Church Cathedral. (There were fourteen nominees, including Kootenay Bishop and Acting Metropolitan Walter Adams, Athabasca's Arthur Sovereign, ATC principal H.R. Trumpour, Father–now Canon–Wilberforce Cooper of St. James's, Canon Harold King of St. Paul's, the newly installed Dean Cecil Swanson of Christ Church Cathedral, and the recently departed Dr. Ramsay Armitage, who had been made principal of Wycliffe College. The contest, which went six ballots, was between Heathcote and Armitage.)

Seventy-two years old when elected, Sir Francis asked "that I may be regarded not only as a Father in God, but as the Elder Brother to all the clergy in the diocese."

"He was a dear man," says Godfrey Gower. "They loved him wherever he went."

Heathcote (Heth-cut) was born in Northamptonshire, a descendant of a family which purchased its estate from Richard III and was given its baronetcy by George II. Young Heathcote attended Lancing College (Evelyn Waugh's school), and then emigrated to Canada. He settled in Peterborough and went to work on a farm. For more than two years, the future baronet bishop wheeled a barrow and sold potatoes at twenty-five cents a sack. ("Youngest son," explains Archbishop Gower. "No patrimony." Not for another fifty-three years.)

Mr. Heathcote studied at Trinity College and was ordained in 1891. He worked in Toronto parishes until 1905, when he became rector of All Saints', Winnipeg. In 1913, he was asked to be Archdeacon of Columbia (the title of the archdeaconry was changed to "Vancouver" in 1924). He moved into offices in the *Vancouver Province* building and served as Archbishop de Pencier's second-in-command for almost four decades.

The newspapermen loved him. "The 6-foot 2-inch cleric is one of the permanent fixtures of The Province Building," wrote Charles King, and looks "no more venerable than a pink-cheeked boy." John Kirkwood called him "the big man with the booming voice and hearty laugh."

O.R. Rowley described him as "a familiar figure as he motors on the roads leading to the various little churches scattered here and there along the Fraser River. His cheery greetings to Saint or Sinner brighten the day for many a traveller. Sometimes, and unawares, he gives a lift to an angel. On a Sunday morning not long ago, he picked up a traveller who dropped off at a prominent golf course, who, unknown to the archdeacon, was the Pro. Within a short time, a great improvement was noted in the archdeacon's game."

And Fred D. Tyner wrote:

You were always the "dignified parson"
As you whirled down our street on your bike
With coat tails all streamin' behind you,
Followed fast by your faithful pup, Mike.

At cricket, you sure were a wizard,
You knocked wickets down with a thud.
When batting, you smiled at the bowler:
"Your name, my dear boy, it is mud."

"He had all kinds of friends," says Godfrey Gower, "bridge friends, golf friends –everybody liked him.

"Once, Camp Artaban needed some lumber for the hall, and it was suggested that perhaps Harvey MacMillan would be interested; so he made an appointment with

Sir Francis Heathcote, fourth Bishop of New Westminster, with confirmation class in Tashme internment camp, 1943. Canon W.H. Gale is fourth from left, top; missionaries Helen Bailey and Frances Hawkins are at far right, centre. Sir Francis was Chairman of Oriental Missions.

Church of the Good Shepherd, 1940. Sir Francis is at the back, towering, as usual, over everyone. Beside Bishop Heathcote stands Hilda Hellaby. By this time, most of the Chinese Anglican children were native Canadians who would grow up, move to the suburbs and attend neighbourhood parish churches.

H.R. MacMillan of MacMillan Bloedel to have lunch at the club. (MacMillan used to sit at a table in the corner, and no member dared sit there.) He and Heathcote met for lunch. 'I suppose you want some lumber,' said MacMillan. 'You can have what you want. Now let's talk about something else.' We got eight or nine thousand dollars worth of lumber."

"He was one of those 'once seen, never forgotten' types," says Hilda Hellaby; "a huge man, with a big, booming voice. He was a strong personality." Sir Francis was Chairman of the Board of Oriental Missions, and Dr. Hellaby worked for him for more than thirty years. Her Chinese friends "were amused by him – but they liked him."

Selwyn Rocksborough-Smith, who came to Burnaby in 1947 to reopen the Borstal school at New Haven, remembers Sir Francis's "great sense of humor. He was quite delightfully amusing – in, perhaps, a rather abrupt way." The jokes he liked best "were his own."

"He belonged to the old Vancouver Round Table, with Spencer, Johnny Jukes, Bell-Irving – that crowd. He always went down to Spencer's for lunch. Went there every day – religiously."

"I've never forgotten him from college," says Archbishop Ted Scott. "He had quite flat feet, and he'd pat-pat-pat down the corridor. You could always tell who was going down. There also used to be a little bit of fun among the students as to who would take the service faster, Dr. Trumpour or Bishop Heathcote. They could rattle through the service at an awful rate."

Perhaps the grandest picture of Sir Francis is David Somerville's: "He liked to go over to Qualicum for holidays. He always went swimming carrying his walking stick and wearing his Panama hat. And he floated, in a stately way, around Qualicum Bay."

"Did you hear what Swanny said last night?" was a frequent Monday morning remark in Vancouver in the 1940s. "Swanny" was Cecil Swanson, Dean of Christ Church Cathedral, and every Sunday he spoke on radio station CJOR. (The Evensong broadcasts were paid for by a trust established by Edward Farmer, and, writes Archdeacon Swanson, they were to be continued "for as long as, in the opinion of the Executive of the Diocese, they were 'doing good work' – truly no lawyer's language.")

David Somerville remembers that "people all over the Northwest listened to [the broadcasts], up the Coast and into the States." Swanson was not only "a marvellous dean" but also a "public performer – and very good at it. His public ministry was the great thing. He was almost the unofficial Chaplain to the City."

Swanson was a Wycliffe man, but his early education was at Dulwich, the school attended by P.G. Wodehouse and Raymond Chandler. He first served in Christ Church in 1920, as curate to Dr. W.W. Craig ("a fine, rather poetic speaker," Swanson remembers.) He returned as dean in 1940, succeeding Ramsay Armitage. (Renison and Sovereign had left the diocese in 1932, after a magnificent dual consecration ceremony in which the first was made Bishop of Athabasca and the second Bishop of Yukon.)

Armitage, writes Swanson, was "a master of the science of liturgics and an indefatigable pastor....He was an old campaigner of the 3rd Battalion CEF and was awarded the Military Cross for his work as a chaplain, and it was natural for him to be appointed Senior Chaplain to the Forces in Vancouver."

Princess Elizabeth at Christ Church Cathedral in 1951. It was Trafalgar Day, and Nelson's signal waved outside the church beside the white ensign. Dean Swanson was a navy man.

In 1943, Armitage was Secretary of General Synod's Prayer Book Revision Committee (thirty years earlier, his father had held the same position). "Typically," notes Archdeacon Swanson, "when asked about a gift [in thanks for his work], he chose an Anglo-Saxon dictionary and...a copy of the Scriptures in the old tongue!"

Dean Swanson was at the centre of historic Vancouver occasions from 1940 until 1953. He conducted the funeral of Senator Gerry McGeer, the city's mayor in the 1930s Depression ("...born in Hogan's Alley... he had a vision of the kind of city Vancouver might become....the cathedral was packed full to the roof. I had asked Tiny Elphicke of CKWX if he could rig up a public address system out to Burrard....the crowd was ten deep along Georgia...and, all the way to the cemetery, as soon as the lights of the lead car came in view, people came running.... men were weeping and women sobbing"). And he welcomed Princess Elizabeth and Prince Philip to the cathedral. ("We presented them with two lovely prayer books, and as I escorted her up the aisle after the service, she whispered, looking at the book in her hand, 'It looks as if I am pinching a book from the church!'")

The Venerable Cecil Swanson published his memoirs in 1977, calling them *The Days of My Sojourning.* One of the celebrated persons he had met when a very young man was Bishop John Dart of New Westminster. The meeting was aboard a ship in mid-Atlantic, and young Swanny was sent to ask the bishop if he would preach at a service. "I found His Lordship," writes Archdeacon Swanson, "in a deckchair wrapped in a blanket. I approached him with timidity and respect, and invited him to come. He looked at me as at a thoroughly undesirable object and muttered two words.

"'Go away,' he said.

"I departed in haste. How could I know he was seasick?

"Fifty years later I took a funeral in the New Westminster cemetery, and at the close of the service I found myself looking at a stately stone memorial marked 'John Dart, Bishop of New Westminster.' I stood there, courteously removed my hat, bowed, and said, 'Go away!'"

Snapshot of Dean Cecil Swanson and Mrs. J.H. King at ceremony commemorating laying of the cornerstone at Christ Church Cathedral by Mrs. King's father, pioneer CPR engineer Lt. Col. Lacey Johnson.

Japanese Canadians were banished from the Pacific Coast in 1942. Missionaries went with them.

Diocesan synods continued to express social concerns in the 1940s. Theo de Pencier moved that a full-time chaplain be appointed for "work in police court and penal and reform institutions." Another motion asked that "a delegation from this synod meet the Minister of Education and urge him to make provisions for the regular reading of portions of the Bible in public schools." But the overwhelming social concern was World War II and the ways it was changing people's lives.

Few Canadian lives were changed as abruptly as those of West Coast Japanese families. Grace Tucker, who had worked in Japanese Missions for the Woman's Auxiliary since 1930, remembers: "December 7, 1941 – the day Japan bombed Pearl Harbor – was Sunday. At 7:00 p.m., we had our regular evening services...a faithful few of the older generation had gathered....stunned by what had happened, anxious, shocked, apprehensive, fearful. What would happen to them and their children? We could reassure them ! This was Canada, and they would receive just and democratic treatment."

"City On War Basis As Pacific Erupts" was the next morning's headline. "British Columbia went to war against Japan Sunday," the story said. "RCMP and Provincial Police swiftly rounded up dangerous enemy aliens while spokesmen for British Columbia's 24,000 Japanese declared their unswerving allegiance to Canada. Japanese language schools and newspapers were closed. A roundup of the Japanese fishing fleet, which will be immobilized, was under way."

Seventy-five per cent of the British Columbia Japanese were Canadian citizens by birth or by naturalization, writes Miss Tucker, but "they had none of the rights of a Canadian. Government by orders-in-council had begun. A dusk to dawn curfew was imposed...cameras, radios, flashlights, cars...were impounded. The Press, the Honourable Members of Parliament, business men, even teachers in the schools joined in a chorus of hate and abuse. I am sorry to report that in this time of opportunity, the voice of the Christian Church was not heard – or was a very faint whisper...."

"There was some deep concern," says Archbishop Scott, "and a lot of deep personal pastoral work done, but that was still at the stage where the church tended to see its work mostly in terms of...ambulance work, after something had happened, rather than raising questions about what the policy was doing. A lot of the people in the missions went out and ministered...but there wasn't much of a hue and cry about the policy position."

Canada invoked the War Measures Act to "relocate" its Japanese citizens in work camps. Hastings Park was used as a "clearing pool." Orders from the British Columbia Security Commission declared: "Persons of Japanese origin residing in Vancouver should terminate...all leases or rental arrangements....They must also be prepared to move either to Hastings Park or to work camps or to places under the Interior Housing Scheme at twenty-four hours notice. No deferments whatsoever...."

"This really meant *all*," says Grace Tucker, "the seriously ill, the crippled, the t.b. patients–everyone. One MP promised 'not one Jap will ever be back in B.C.'"

At Hastings Park, families were crowded into cattle stalls. Canon W.H. Gale conducted a service of Holy Communion in the barns. Hundreds of small children were there, from as far away as Prince Rupert. Margaret Foster, who had been a kindergarten teacher for the Japanese community since leaving Trinity College in 1929, worked with other Anglican and United Church women to organize school classes. "You had to have a pass to get in," she says. "And when I'd go there in the morning, my bags were searched, to make sure I wasn't taking a camera. Well," she smiles, "of *course* I was taking a camera." Many of her photographs (taken with "a little old box camera given me by my prayer partner when I left Toronto") are now part of the permanent record of those years of evacuation and internment.

"I think it's agreed now," says Archbishop Scott, "there was never any real need for them to be moved, but the war situation provided a focus for the negative, anti-Japanese attitudes to be raised at that time, and there were some pretty brutal aspects to that...there was so much vandalism on the fishing boats that were left."

When Japanese families were exiled from Vancouver, the men and women who had been working in Japanese missions went with them. "They weren't going to send us," says Grace Tucker. "We had a bit of a battle."

By 1943, there were Japanese Anglican communities in Slocan City, New Denver, Salmon Arm, Kamloops and Tashme. Some were in road camps. Others were in ghost towns. Seven thousand Japanese were placed in the Slocan area. "People were coming up so fast," Miss Tucker remembers, "they had

"Dangerous enemies of the state" present a Nativity pageant at Slocan City internment camp.

Internment camp school built at Bayfarm, Slocan City, 1943. Project was directed by Genji Suzuki (eighth from right, front), grandfather of geneticist David—also in camp. G.G.Nakayama is far right, front; to his left is Hattie Horobim; Margaret Foster is fourth from right.

to get old American Army tents. We had hundreds of people under canvas when the snows came. The first baby was born in one of those tents."

The minister at Slocan was the Reverend Gordon Goichi Nakayama, who had come from Kyoto to Vancouver in 1919. A Buddhist youth, he had been converted to Christianity while listening to Father Cooper one Good Friday.

"Father Cooper," writes Timothy Nakayama, Gordon Nakayama's son, "was conducting meditations on the Stations of the Cross. He had come to the scene where the Lord was speaking from the Cross to his Blessed Mother and to St. John, 'Woman, behold thy son: son, behold thy mother.' Fr. Cooper was explaining in his own inimitable way the beautiful love of our Saviour and how he expressed it, even in his hour of agony, in his concern for his mother and the beloved disciple.

'Up to this point, Nakayama, like many Japanese, because of their history and culture, had believed that Christianity had stood for all that was bad in individualism and selfishness, with an utter disregard of family life and filial piety. Now, in the supreme act of Christ in his love manifested

Kindergarten graduation at Bayfarm. Teachers are Margaret Foster and Aya Tokunaga, top left, and Kay Nishimura, right. "The little ones enjoyed it," says Miss Foster. "They had fun."

Camp women formed a branch of the Woman's Auxiliary and met with Slocan colleagues. Mrs. Popoff, Mayor of Slocan City, stands far left. Next to her are Margaret Foster, Slocan W.A. President Mrs. Parker, and Aya Suzuki. Grace Tucker sits at centre, Mrs. Nakayama on her left.

towards his mother, as Fr. Cooper expressed it, the young Japanese found the wonderful experience of Christian peace, joy, hope and love."

Gordon Nakayama was baptized a Christian. He married Lois Masui Yao, who had come from the Kindergarten Teachers' Training School of the Nippon Seikokai to work at the Church of the Ascension. He entered the Anglican Theological College and became the parish's lay reader. He was ordained in 1932. Eleven years later, he would travel the country comforting uprooted Japanese Canadians.

"In the interior towns," wrote Timothy Nakayama, "the government provided, after some procrastination, elementary education, but high schools were not provided and the Church took the opportunity to fill the need. At Slocan City the mission established a high school with Miss Nora Bowman as principal. Miss Bowman...had been matron in charge of St. Mary's Girls' School and Hostel in Matsumoto. Assisting her were Miss Hattie M. Horobin and Miss Elsie Heaps. Also active in the work of the Mission at Slocan was Miss Alice M. Cox who, for forty years, had been a missionary of the CMS. She spoke Japanese fluently and was able to enter fully into the lives of the people. Miss Margaret Foster, an energetic and cheerful worker, did much for the children of kindergarten age. Miss Grace Tucker was invaluable in maintaining a liaison between the government and the people."

Other workers in the new Japanese Canadian communities were Aya Suzuki and Gertrude Shore in Slocan; Kathleen Lang in Kamloops; Florence Hamilton, Miss M. Clench and the Reverend F. Brown in New Denver; the Reverend Reginald Savary, based in Salmon Arm, and travelling between Sicamous and Revelstoke; and Canon William Gale, Frances Hawkins, Helen Bailey, Mae Waller and Shizue Naka in Tashme, where 2,600 Japanese lived, thirteen miles from Hope.

"Our idea," writes Grace Tucker, "was to do everything we could to bring happiness under these very difficult conditions, so picnics, hikes and other gatherings were arranged. We tried to stress the bright future...." But the future wasn't bright. "Very early, it became clear that the policy of the government was to move the people out of B.C. into other provinces....Early in 1945 the Department of Labor began a campaign to "send them back to Japan, apparently overlooking the fact that they had never been there."

"The first place we went from Slocan was Neys, a German prison camp on Lake Superior," says Margaret Foster. Second-generation and third-generation Canadian Japanese lived in this maximum security POW camp behind eight-foot-high barbed wire fences, in rough wooden huts, under the continuous glare of floodlights. Eventually, the community of West Coast Japanese was allowed to go north to Crow Creek, near Kapuskasing, to work in black spruce bush camps. Margaret Foster went with them.

Meanwhile, in Toronto, Grace Tucker and Aya Suzuki were meeting trains from the B.C. Interior, helping the Japanese aboard to start building new lives in Eastern Canada.

Two years after the war, the Japanese still couldn't travel freely in Canada. Many of their possessions had been sold for fractions of their value, or destroyed. Some of the Japanese returned to British Columbia. Some went to Japan. The majority resettled in Eastern Canada. But wherever they are, they remember the women who went into exile with them, the women they called *Sensei* (teacher).

In her collection of poems, *A Choice of Dreams,* Joy Kogawa writes: "What do I remember of the evacuation? I remember

John Antle at the London docks ready to sail to Vancouver via the Panama Canal.

Miss Foster and Miss Tucker...who did what they could/And loved the children and who gave me/A puzzle to play with on the train."

"I shall never forget the end of the war," writes Cecil Swanson. "A radio station called at 7:00 A.M. to say that the war was over, and what were we going to do about it? I said, 'We shall hold a service of thanksgiving at 11 o'clock and other similar services on the hour for as long as there were people wanting them.' In the evening, we had an enormous congregation, packing the church, and, among other things, we played all the national anthems of the united nations, or at least as many as we could find. I remember Paul Jocelin, the United States Consul General, calling me to say that while he had heard *The Star Spangled Banner* played by The Marines' Band...nothing could be compared to the glorious playing of the anthem by Frederick Chubb. We didn't know the Dutch anthem, so we played *We Gather Together to Ask the Lord's Blessing.* We sang *O Canada,* of course, and then wiped them all out with *God Save the King!*"

War's end brought another kind of work for the church. "I had girls come to me," says Archdeacon Swanson, "saying that they didn't even know the men they had married." Men who had been chaplains returned to help pick up the pieces of emotional debris. One of these men was the Reverend W.C. "Dan" Daniel, ATC 1927, who had worked as a Sea Island and Jericho Beach chaplain to men in uniform, and now worked as a rehabilitation officer with men in civvies. "There was no welfare then," he says, "and people came to us with their problems."

Deaconess Hilda Hellaby's thirty years of work in Chinese missions ended. One summer, Archbishop Adams, administering the Diocese of Yukon as well as Kootenay, needed someone to run a children's hostel. The job paid sixty dollars a month and room and board. Dean Swanson suggested that she go for the summer. The next year, she found herself looking after the parish church and school in the Indian village of Mayo. "Travelling several miles a day through bush and over frozen rivers," she wrote, "was a far cry from the East End of Vancouver." Two years passed. "You can't go back two years later and say, 'move over, I'm back'" says Dr. Hellaby. "It seemed the thing to do to stay on." She's been in the Yukon ever since.

"Eight bells chimed from the stern of the Columbia Coast Mission flagship *Columbia,*" reported the *Vancouver Sun,* "and the body of the Reverend John Antle was committed to 120 fathoms in Manson's Deep." The sailor-priest had died at 84, December 3, 1949. The Reverend Alan Greene, who had followed him as superintendent of the Mission, conducted the burial service at sea. An escort of powerboats from the Royal Vancouver Yacht Club accompanied the *Columbia* and an RVYC guard of honor stood at the stern. Captain Antle had helped form the club, and it was in its basin, aboard his yacht *Reverie,* that his final illness had come.

Dr. Honor Kidd wrote a tribute to John Antle in *The Canadian Medical Association Journal:* "It is impossible to detail all the activities of the Columbia Coast Mission. The marine ambulance service was the most dramatic part of its work, but among other things it undertook annual medical examinations of school children, conducted outpost clinics, started dental clinics, gave pre- and post-natal care and established well-baby clinics for Indian mothers.... The Alert Bay hospital was of particular benefit to the Indians. The number of Indian maternity cases admitted increased steadily and there was a consequent reduction in infant mortality and improved child health."

On October 31, 1950, Sir Francis Heathcote resigned his episcopacy. He was 83 years old. A reporter telephoned him on his birthday to ask how he was. "I'm getting grouchier than ever!" boomed the bishop.

"How," asks Godfrey Gower, "could you help but love a bishop like that?"

Bishop Heathcote and Canon John Leigh. The Grand Old Man strolls down Hastings into history.

Part III

Visions and Reality

Men stay in the church because they know empirically that the sacraments provide the food and drink of a life of communion and illumination. All the rest is distraction . . . It is the life that counts, and I for one refuse to be distracted from that life, although I may be sufficiently exasperated in the mundane world by the specific sectarian absurdities of the church.

— Kenneth Rexroth
Faith in an Age of Faithlessness

People are people. Holiness stays the same.
— Herbert O'Driscoll

Changing of the shepherd: Sir Francis Heathcote and Godfrey Gower at the consecration of the fifth Bishop of New Westminster on the Feast of the Conversion of Paul in 1951.

The sixth decade of the twentieth century started deceptively, as though nothing much had changed, despite two world wars and one world depression. But a spiritual malaise hung over society, like fallout, and the only value system unshaken was one of acquisitiveness. None of this would be generally acknowledged until the sharp violence of the 1960s threw it into focus, and by that time Kenneth Rexroth's warning would be almost too late: "When a culture loses its interiority, when the tiny flame of contemplation in the heart of civilization goes out, chaos and death take over."

The church was identified with the social system. It adhered to order and authority, as St. Paul had told it to. The great decision for the church during North America's mid-life crisis was whether to remain a subordinate community institution, or to become once again the obstreperous prophet, a disturbance in the king's court. And the moment when this decision was forced upon the church in Canada came when the Right Reverend Ralph Dean, of the Anglican Communion, told General Synod that the church's days could be numbered. He gave it another ten years before it might "die of self-strangulation...throttled by its own prosperity."

Many of the ways in which the church struggled to retain its stature in society (to be relevant, in the jargon of the period) were naive and silly. It was trying desperately to keep up, as may be seen in these headlines from diocesan papers:

"What is the Church's Answer to the Computer?"

"Transplants a Moral Problem?"

"Did Jesus Reject a Chance to Become a Swinger?"

But all of this was to come in the 1960s. In the 1950s, it was business as usual.

On the Feast of the Conversion of St. Paul, January 25, 1951, Godfrey Philip Gower was consecrated fifth Lord Bishop of New Westminster. The sermon was preached by the Reverend Douglas Watney, the ATC professor who was to become Bishop Gower's effective long-time archdeacon—his Horatio figure.

Once again, there had been enough episcopal nominees to field a football team: thirteen, including Ramsay Armitage, Cecil Swanson, Alan Greene of the Columbia Coast Mission, Dudley Kemp, Archdeacon James Thomson, and a quartet of men who were already bishops—W.L. Wright, Algoma (Archbishop de Pencier's nephew); R.H. Waterman, Nova Scotia; H.R. "Harry" Ragg, Calgary (who had been rector of St. Thomas's, Chilliwack, in the 1920s and returned to the Diocese of New Westminster on his retirement to be Bishop Gower's honorary assistant); and Walter Barfoot, Edmonton (who lost this election but won his next one and became Primate). Despite the plethora of candidates, Godfrey Gower was chosen on the second ballot.

The new bishop had been born fifty-one years earlier in Sturmer, Sussex. "My boyhood," he writes, "was spent in a small village in Essex and there I used to play the organ for services in a church which had a record of its clergy as far back as 1347. Previous to that it had been a shrine where charcoal burners in the oak forests used to worship."

He was a Royal Flying Corps pilot in World War I and then graduated as a mechanical engineer from the Imperial College of Science and Technology. In 1925 he came to Canada and studied at the Vermilion School of Agriculture. For two years, he worked at the Dominion Experimental Farm at Beaver Lodge in the Peace River Country.

In 1927, he went to Edmonton for Christmas and to arrange to enter the School of Sciences at the University of Alberta. But instead, he met Henry Allan Gray, Bishop of Edmonton ("If it's a question of head or heart, use your heart; bring your head in later") and instead of going to the University of Alberta, he went to St. John's College in Winnipeg. He was ordained in 1930.

Gower worked in various Alberta parishes until World War II, serving last as rector of Christ Church, Edmonton. Then he joined the RCAF as a chaplain, and was posted to Europe with the rank of squadron leader. In 1944, he came to Vancouver and the old Yaletown church, St. Paul's in the West End. (Archbishop de Pencier still worshipped in the church where he'd been rector. Gower always said to him, 'Your Grace, put your robes on and sit in the sanctuary.' He loved that.)

Bishop Gower identified the Great Enemy in his first charge to synod. Quoting Sir Alexander Clutterbuck, he said, "The struggle today is not primarily political or economic. The struggle is a spiritual one and the prize for the victor is the Soul of Man." An eternally avant garde perception, recalling John Dart's warnings about the secularization of life and similar aphorisms two milleniums old; but the world at large viewed the struggle as entirely political or economic, with the Soul of Man an incidental prize, like the toy ring in the box of Crackerjack.

Notes from "A Bishop's Diary," 1954:

"Jan. 3rd–A great day and a fine start for the new year. Preached at Lynn Valley to two congregations in the one church, sensing a real fellowship amongst the people. Attended the Memorial Service at the Cathedral for the victims of the train disaster in New Zealand and preached. This was requested by the crew of the *Waruna*. Everyone deeply moved, and I found words were difficult. On to St. Agnes', North Vancouver, in the evening, where the church was full in spite of pouring rain.

"Jan. 6th–Spent Epiphanytide with the Young People at the 7:00 a.m. Holy Communion at the Cathedral. Surprised to see the Chapel full. Confirmation of adults at the old picturesque church of St. Mary's, Sapperton.

"Jan. 10th–A glorious day and the Fraser Valley a rhapsody in blue and white–a fleeting beauty before the long dark stormy days. Preached at Chilliwack on the Privilege of Witness.

"Jan. 11th–17th–What a week! Monday full of interviews–reflecting at the end of the day on the Fourth Commandment and wondering whether I am not continually breaking it. Tuesday another long stretch in the office and an adult confirmation service at St. Philip's–spoke on Personal Witness and took heart from the young men in front of me. A crowded church and an uplift at St. John's, Central Park, on Wednesday evening, where we dedicated a restored and improved church. Happy to see the bright interior replacing the sombre brown–remembering there is a Rainbow round the Throne in *Revelation*. Thursday a day of meeting and detail; grateful for an Archdeacon who is not only the Bishop's Eye but also his memory. Friday comes and again the sweep of Church activities before me, Camp Artaban and the Prayer Book Revision, Parish Committee. Saturday and a rest, looking forward to my service with the men at Shaughnessy Hospital and at St. Faith's on Sunday evening. Walked the wards with Padre Ramsey, feeling grateful to him for his ministry there.

"Jan. 18th–24th–Privileged to say Grace at luncheon on board the *Oronsay* and in the evening spoke to the United Services Institute on 'Canada and the Twentieth Century.' The audience were most kind and no investigation committee has subpoenaed me yet! On Wednesday attended the Cathedral for the 6:30 Supper Club and heard Percy White on Korea. Presided at the Annual Meeting of Camp Artaban listening to a grand record of youth work....Saturday, snow–chains–shovelling–'most unusual weather for Vancouver' but it did not daunt the congregation of St. Saviour's on Sunday morning where once again we felt a Presence.

"Jan. 25–31st–Meetings of the House of Bishops, remembering the anniversary of Bishop Heathcote's consecration and also my own. Somewhat chastened at the thought and asked myself some very personal questions. How good to see the Bishops of the

Yukon and Caledonia undismayed by their frustrations. Patrick Kootenay delayed by snow slides, turned up late. Bishops are like other people, hard to manage and so reluctant to concentrate on the business at hand. They have so much on their episcopal chests which they must get off. Good meetings next day with College Executive. We have a magnificent opportunity to make our College the seminary of the Pacific North-West. Why not also a School of Oriental Studies? On Wednesday we went to the Lord's Day Alliance Meeting haunted by the thought that you cannot legislate a man into religion and wishing the Lord's Day Act could be revised to meet modern conditions. Thursday was brightened by a conference on Columbia Coast Mission matters with that tough sailor and gentle Christian, Alan Greene. The fog descends and my movements are shrouded in darkness. Almost a lost weekend but enjoyed sitting in a pew for once.

"Feb. 1st–8th–When the fog lifts I am with the North Vancouver Missions to Seamen. Learned we serve 22,000 seamen a year through our three centres....On Tuesday we discussed Christian Education at a Deanery meeting. Wednesday found us in church with

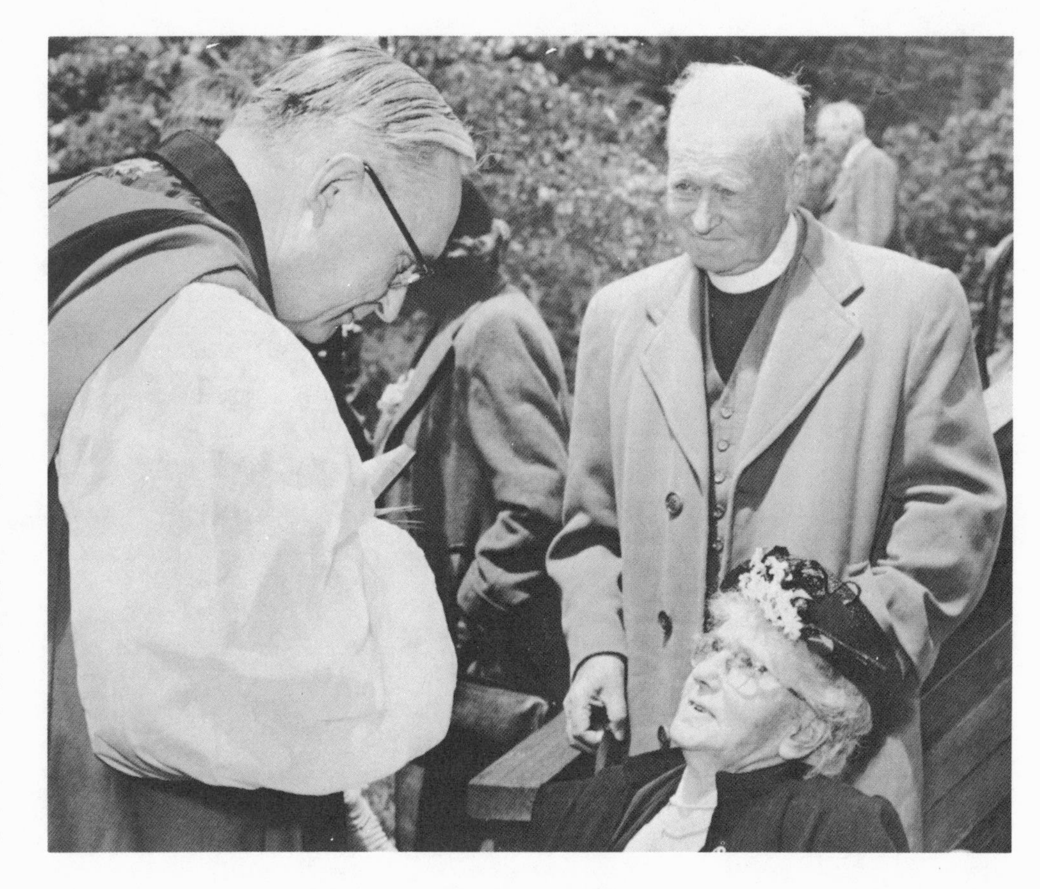

Primate Walter Barfoot greets Harriet Woodward in 1954 at St. John the Divine, Yale. Miss Woodward had been a teacher at All Hallows' School in Sillitoe's era, sixty years earlier.

The Editor asks for an article written
  Of history? humour?—the length left to me,
Recording impressions with which I was smitten
  In the long, lurid past of renowned A.T.C.

There is childhood's remembrance of students so eager
  Progressing to Christ Church from Latimer Hall,
While others, more spiky, disciples of Seager,
  En route from St. Mark's to the Church of St. Paul.

Or later, when wartime privation of dollars
  Has welded them both in amalgamate mass:
Professors who differ, and schizophrene scholars
  Assundered on questions of candles at Mass.

Years pass, and, a student with pious ambitions
  (Windows wide to the blare of Point Atkinson's horn),
I find the "amalgam" has jelled to conditions—
  All churchmanship shades for the time must conform!

Great days of Bill Vance, the keen-tongued bubble-buster,
  Of Trumpour and Shortt and of Keeling so round,
While of Heresey Hill, Scott and Sanford add lustre—
  O. T. and R. E., fruit of learning profound.

Years later, one springtime I go to a meeting,
  (Alumni: disposal of funds to debate)
And there in amazement I find myself greeting
  Old men of demeanour both grave and sedate.

There is X---, when last seen, a freshly-hatched Deacon,
  Now a Ven.; and just over his shoulder, I see
(Who used to be slim as a straight traffic-beacon)
  None other than Y---, now a paunchy D.D.

And so, 'midst the ribaldries, Canons are roaring
  To baldheads and greyheads erstwhile young as I,
(As innocent, too) till the truth, inward boring,
  Strikes deep to evoke from heart's anguish a cry:

"If I look like they look,
They're probably thinking
That they look like I look—
I hope they're not right.

But if they feel like I feel
Then surely they're thinking
That I feel like they feel—
The outlook's more bright!"

E.W.J.

Anglican Theological College's golden anniversary moved Canon E.W. Jackson to nostalgic verse.

The 75th anniversary of the birth of the diocese was marked in 1954 by a pilgrimage to Bishop Sillitoe's grave. Primate Barfoot is second from right. Smoking mills and factories line the Fraser River in the background.

some dear boys and girls at a confirmation at St. Francis'. On Thursday, St. Catherine's, Capilano, presented plans for dealing with accommodation for 500 children. Friday afternoon, I visited the hospital. I hope the patients realize I felt much better after the visit. Tried to settle down on Saturday to do some reading, and found it hard going and diagnosed my condition as anticipatory bursitis (an ache in the bones to get going on Sunday). Sunday, 9:30 a.m.—Confirmation in the B.C. Penitentiary before some hundred men. Then on to St. Thomas', Whalley, speaking on Christlikeness which I need more than they. Then to St. Stephen's, West Van., for another confirmation for 30 boys and girls—fine well-prepared group. What possibilities we have amongst our youth!"

Bishop Gower confirmed more than twenty thousand children and adults. He calls them his "children in Christ" and says, "I regard those people as part of my family and myself as part of theirs." To children, at confirmation services, he liked to say, "Christianity is like tea: It lifts you up and it never lets you down."

He spoke more sternly in the city outside the church: "Many people live as if there were no God at all," he said. "In this affluent economy most of us have the means to satisfy our whims....This imposes a greater onus upon the individual to discipline himself." He urged "a separation of self from everyday affairs, a time of healthy self-examination and of spiritual rest. But this is what many men and women are afraid to do. They are afraid to be quiet. They are afraid to look at themselves....Instead, they rush to become joiners, to run with the crowd at all costs. They keep up a frenzied activity because if they put the world aside, even momentarily, what's to take its place but emptiness?

"If we starve our spirits," he warned, "we depersonalize ourselves and decrease the grandeur of our stature as human beings."

At Christmastide, 1960, he said, "The church has a long-term view. Its task is to change people's hearts....The church was established by martyrs who proclaimed the truth to those who would not hear it or rejected it. For centuries the church was the repository of truth and knowledge when man generally was yielding himself to violent impulses and actions....The world must understand that the church cannot be neutral when truth is attacked."

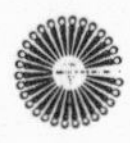

On a September day in 1961, Bishop Gower spoke at the funeral of Sir Francis Heathcote: "This humble-minded man, who answered the call to the ministry with such diffidence, stands in the succession of the truly great men of God who have enriched the life of the whole Canadian Church. They were men who knew themselves chosen to lead and to build, fearful only that their own weakness might betray the trust laid upon them."

The visit to the Diocese by Dr. Geoffrey Fisher, Archbishop of Canterbury (centre, left). Beside Dr. Fisher is Vancouver Mayor Fred Hume. Smiling faces at left belong to Bishop Gower and Metropolitan Harold Sexton.

In 1966, the Chapel of the Epiphany at ATC was consecrated by Archbishop Harold Sexton, Metropolitan of British Columbia. Godfrey Gower spoke, saying, "Christianity is a living and thus a changing and renewing thing. It is a way of walking and not of talking, a divine light and not a divine science. Its garments, liturgical or otherwise, can be folded up and put away. It can assume new dress. But the truth enshrined in the Gospel is timeless and beyond change. We need to determine the difference between the fixed and unchanging and what is changeable."

Later that year, Archbishop Sexton returned to the Chapel on the University of British Columbia campus to consecrate Ted Scott as Bishop of Kootenay.

Diocesan synod in April, 1966, approved an historic motion by Mr. Justice T.G. Norris and Mr. J.W. Lane of St. John's, Maple Ridge with Pitt Meadows: "the removal of all discriminatory powers against women in the appointment or election to office in the work of the Church." New Westminster became the fourteenth diocese in Canada to "give the vote to women." The *Anglican News* headline: "You Made It, Ladies!"

At UBC, Anglican Chaplain Alan Jackson

stepped into the explosive "God is dead" controversy, saying he doubted the existence of a God "as we have been taught to know him."

The very phrase "God is dead" (it appeared dead centre on a black *Time* magazine cover) was devastating to people of the mid-sixties. They didn't want metaphysical speculation, they wanted certainties. They were not calmed by Bishop Gower's reassurance: "What I think these people are saying is this, there is a need to present the idea of God in terms that are relevant to modern man." Fury broke loose in the *Anglican News* letters column. Jackson resigned.

"I would have said the same thing," Jackson said, as he left UBC (to become, in the 1970s, Dean of St. Saviour's Pro-Cathedral at Nelson in the Diocese of Kootenay), "but I would have said it in different language."

Some priests defended Jackson and regretted his leaving. At St. Alban the Martyr, Dudley Ritchie said, "He was making a real contribution to the ferment of thought that is now taking place...."

John Bishop, the first Anglican chaplain at UBC, later rector of St. John the Divine, said, "We need more people, not less, involved

Dr. Jim Cruickshank of the Vancouver School of Theology with wife Sue, children Jason and Anna. Cruickshank was first director of Sorrento Centre, "an island of the future," in the 1960s.

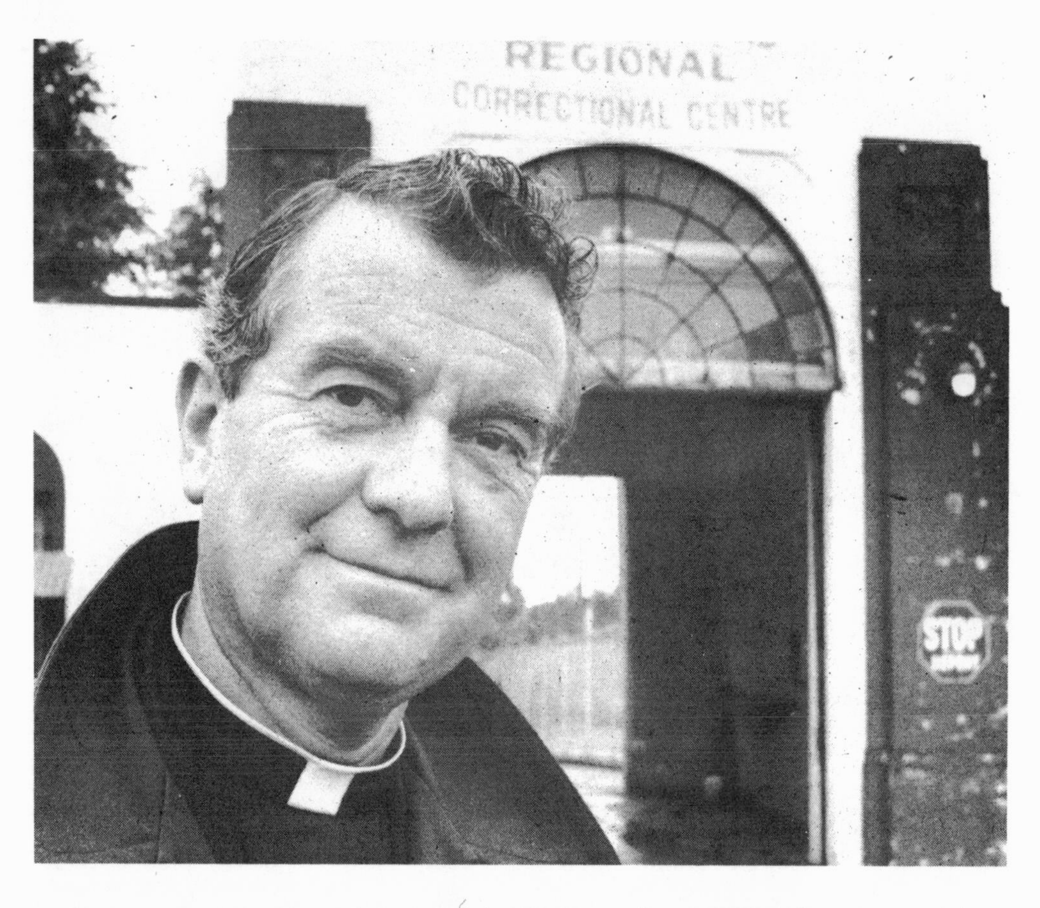

Father Edward Hulford became Oakalla chaplain in 1965. He coordinated 1968 Oakalla conference of clergy, laity and corrections officials to consider alternatives to the present criminal justice system.

in open dialogue....a university chaplain must be given support and freedom....until we work at this level...any chaplain worth his salt will be in trouble. Talking with many university people, I find them confessing a real doubt that the Anglican Church can meet this situation. This is the real issue and dilemma."

Four hundred miles from UBC, on the shore of Shuswap Lake, a young priest from Prince George was developing a centre called Sorrento where laymen could be trained to "carry out the work of the church in the world." His name was Jim Cruickshank, and he said, "God is not dead, nor is He up there on a pink cloud. God is everywhere and if you will let Him, He will teach others through you."

One of the priests who worked at St. James's in the early 1950s was Edward Hulford, who had been a server in the skid road parish while attending UBC. When he moved into the clergy house, he says, "I thought to myself, this is where I belong."

And, said Father Cooper, he "proved to be a remarkably able shepherd of souls.

I've never known greater patience than his in dealing with the most difficult down-and-outs. Whether it were such a one, or some wild gang of boys, or a very sick person, Father Hulford gave liberally of his skill and care....We used to say, 'Go on, Eddie, put your white coat on,' for at Toronto they had given theological students a course in clinical psychology."

Often Eddie Hulford went to court with his people and helped supervise their probation. For four years he was chaplain at Haney Correctional Centre. In 1965, he became chaplain at Oakalla Prison. Eventually, he would be named director of religious programs for the British Columbia corrections branch.

On the waterfront, Father Clinton's Missions to Seamen continued to welcome sailors from around the world. Canon Stanley Smith nightly said the Lord's Prayer in seven languages. (Daytimes he worked at building a bowling alley and dance floor. The inaugural bowling match was to be between Bishop Gower and the port manager, Captain Barney Johnson. "If they are both telling the truth," said Canon Smith, "this should be pretty awful bowling to watch, but I have a feeling they are hiding their light beneath a bushel.")

In the basement of St. James's, a retired Burnaby social worker named William Meal started a club for pensioners. When it began, in 1958, most of the members were grizzled old bachelors who had spent their working days as prospectors or ranchers or farmers. When they closed up their cabins, they came to Vancouver and moved into rooming houses to live on the money they'd managed to save. Government pensions were small then and there were few social assistance programs. These pensioners, says May Gutteridge, were "a very different breed—bathing and that sort of thing wasn't very important—but they had great tales to tell you of their life in the bush."

May Gutteridge had come to Canada from England in 1955 with her teacher husband and three children. They went first to Prairie River, thirty miles from Hudson's Bay. "It was high adventure," she says. "I just fell in love with Canada." In 1960, she began work in the basement of St. James's. "Then I was asked by the bishop if I would get involved with Indian people." She said she would try it, to find out "if they liked me and I liked them." Inspector Hewitt of the Vancouver Police Women's Division arranged for Mrs. Gutteridge to visit Oakalla every Tuesday. The Indian women there did like her. And she liked them.

"All I did," she says, "is what you would do for anybody—pick up clothes, write letters, get in touch with relations." The visits were held in Hut 2, where the Indian women lived. "They used to make tea and bake a cake or cookies. I learned a tremendous amount about the northern reservations and what happened there. It was a very happy time for me."

Back in Vancouver, she tried to be a friend in the city for the Indian women. "Now you know where I am," she'd say, "come and see me. But they were very, very shy, very alienated from the white way of life." If they were found drunk on the streets, they were sent back to jail.

"Indian people couldn't get social assistance then. They weren't eligible. A lot of times, girls would go with any man that gave them shelter, and then they were abused." When welfare money was made available for Indians, the authorities refused to give it directly to them. But they would give the cheques to Mrs. Gutteridge; she became a channel for the funds.

The Rev. Eric Powell baptizing an Indian infant at Kingcome. When Margaret Craven wrote *I Heard the Owl Call My Name*, she based her main character on the experiences of Eric Powell.

One day she went with a group of Anglican Church Women to hear a missionary nurse speak. "The missionary told us that eight Indian girls had died [in Vancouver] and there wasn't even a record of it anywhere. I couldn't understand why all the women didn't stand on their feet and scream."

May Gutteridge decided to open a hostel where Indian women could stay in the city. She formed the East Enders' Society and went looking for a building. She found one in the 800 block on Hastings—a house that had been built for an inspector of the police, then been used by a bootlegger and finally turned into a rooming house. The problem for the East Enders was coming up with the $1,400 down payment. Money just wasn't there, although the society had asked people of the diocese to pledge one dollar a month to help skid road women.

Then Mrs. Gutteridge learned that a new episcopal residence was to be built: Bishopthorpe on West Forty-ninth Avenue. The cost of construction would be more than $68,000. Revenue from the sale of the old residence on Balfour would provide almost half of this, and the diocese intended Bishopthorpe to be not just a residence, but also a centre of diocesan group activities. Even so,

Mrs. Gutteridge was furious.

"I was still in the basement of the church at that time, and the priests came down, and I said to them, 'I think this is terrible—$70,000 going to be spent on a house and we can't even raise $1,400 for a hostel. For two pins, I'd picket your synod!'

"Father Gardiner said, 'Okay.'

"I said, 'You would have a red face if I did.'

"He said, 'I wouldn't worry.'

"So I said it to Father Wright, and he said, 'No, I wouldn't worry.'

"So Alex, our janitor, he made me a wooden thing. I thought, 'I'll pray for three days. I don't know how I'll know, but I'll just keep going very slowly.' I'm very, very cautious and conscious that I must never do anything that will bring disrepute to the church, to the body of the church, to Christ.

"So I hid the wooden thing in a cottage we have at the back of the yard, because my husband wouldn't understand me doing that kind of thing—he's very reserved.

"The next morning I got up early. It was a lovely morning. I had this big paper which I stapled over [the wooden thing]. I went out in the garden and there were some flowers, so I picked them and stapled them around the edge. I put it in the back of my car, and I didn't even know then if I would.

"I got over to [St. John's, Shaughnessy, where synod was sitting], and I thought, 'Guide me. If I'm to do it, I'll do it. I'm frightened, but I'll do it.' And I got it out and I started and I just walked up and down."

Mrs. Gutteridge got money for her hostel, but not from synod. It came from "a United Church lady who wanted to work with us ...she and her sister had just come into some money."

The East Enders bought "a lovely old bay house" and made it ready for their visitors. The first year, four hundred Indian women stayed at the hostel. On its first anniversary, "Dear Dr. Ross of the United Church and Father Gardiner and all the people came and we had a real garden party."

In 1967, a small book called *I Heard the Owl Call My Name* was published. Its author was Margaret Craven, an American writer, who had gone to Kingcome Inlet at the invitation of the Reverend Eric Powell. She dedicated her novel to "the Tsawataineuk

British Columbia Lt. Gov. John Nicholson, Chief David Dawson, and Bishop Gower at Kingcome.

Kingcome Inlet villagers gather outside longhouse to perform Dance of Life for visiting Lt. Gov. George Pearkes. Dedication of Kingcome totem pole by Archbishop de Pencier in 1939 had influenced the British Columbia government to allow Indians to restore ancient rites and symbols.

Tribe at Kingcome Village, B.C. and...Eric Powell."

The novel is about a young priest, just ordained, who has only three years to live. His bishop says, "So short a time to learn so much?....I shall send him to my hardest parish. I shall send him to Kingcome on patrol of the Indian villages." The book has been very popular, especially in the Diocese of New Westminster. It is in the B.C. English curriculum for grade eight, and the story became even more widely known when it was filmed by Daryl Duke. When people learn that Powell was the priest at Kingcome when Craven was there, they're surprised to find him still alive.

"I sent Eric to Kingcome," says Godfrey Gower. "But I didn't send him up there to die."

What did concern Bishop Gower was the young priest's dubious mobility. Powell had just spent six months in hospital and eighteen months in a body cast.

"It was in Smithers," he says. "I was a theological student, working for forestry during the summer months. I was in a jeep. It was the day of my brother's wedding and I was going in from Houston over a dirt road to send him a telegram. There were three of us in the car. We went off a bridge and dropped about eighty-five feet."

All the men survived, although severely injured. "I walked about a mile and a half for help," says Powell. "I managed to find a farmhouse. They flew the others to Vancouver. They thought I was okay." For the next half-year he was paralyzed.

Today, Eric Powell is Director of Program for the diocese. Occasionally he'll go to schools and talk about the culture of the Indian people. Kingcome families come to his office in Vancouver, and he spends fishing holidays up the coast with them. He has, says Godfrey Gower, "a great way of getting the confidence of Indians."

In Duke's film, Tom Courtenay plays the doomed priest and Dean Jagger plays the wise bishop. After the film was shown on television, a friend ran into Archbishop Gower in White Rock. "Say," he said, "was that bishop supposed to be you?"

"I suppose so," said Archbishop Gower. "He had my cope and mitre on."

"Well," said the man, "he looked much better in them than you do."

Kingcome's Ernie Willie, the diocese's first Indian priest, National Human Rights Consultant.

Dean Herbert O'Driscoll of Christ Church Cathedral, to many Canadians in the 1970s one of the prophets of the age. "All of us," he says, "are wrestling with visions."

The new Dean of Christ Church Cathedral, installed in 1968, was T. Herbert O'Driscoll. "He comes to this city with a reputation as a silver-tongued orator," wrote *Anglican News*, "in the best tradition of his Irish forebears."

Born in Cork, O'Driscoll was educated at Trinity College, Dublin, and priested in the cathedral where Jonathan Swift had been dean. He moved to Canada, served two years as a Royal Canadian Navy chaplain, then worked in Ottawa parish churches. The last was St. John the Evangelist, which had been the charge of the man he succeeded as dean, the Very Reverend Northcote Burke.

In the same year of Herbie O'Driscoll's installation as Dean, Godfrey Gower was installed as Metropolitan of the Archdiocese of British Columbia, succeeding the Most Reverend Harold Sexton of Victoria. Around him that day was an extraordinary company of men whose careers were linked to the Diocese of New Westminster: Bishop Ralph Dean of Cariboo and his chaplain, Eric Powell; Bishop Ted Scott of Kootenay; Bishop Eric Munn of Caledonia and his chaplain, Don Dodman; and Archdeacon Douglas Watney.

The Woman's Auxiliary held its first meeting in Canada in 1885. The first New Westminster branch was organized in 1890. In 1967, the W.A. changed its name to Anglican Church Women. This photograph shows delegates to that year's provincial conference held at Christ Church Cathedral, Victoria.

Bishop Gower and Roman Catholic Archbishop Johnson at consecration of Bishop James Carney.

Archbishop Gower's great struggle through almost fifteen years of his episcopate was for union between the Anglican and United Churches in Canada. Each of these churches had appointed a committee to work on the project. Together, these committees formed the General Commission, responsible for drafting a plan of union to be presented to the national bodies for consideration. Archbishop Gower was chairman of the Anglican group (called the Committee on Christian Unity and the Church Universal). Its members included Archdeacon Watney and the Primate, Archbishop Howard Clark. The United Church group included the Right Reverend Wilfred C. Lockhart, President A.B.B. Moore and the Reverend George Morrison of Vancouver's Ryerson United Church.

In countries from New Zealand to Nigeria, the mood of the period was towards ecumenism. In this diocese, the Reverend Roger Maggs said, "It is essential we should be all one in Christ. This is not our own choice, but Christ is calling us to this today." Headlines in *Anglican News* reflected some concerns—"Episcopacy Thorny Problem," and "Will Anglicans Disappear?"—but concluded "Christ Meant Church to be One."

General Synod convened in Vancouver in 1965. Primate Clark concelebrated the eucharist with the Metropolitan of the Church of India, Pakistan, Burma and Ceylon and the Supreme Bishop of the Philippine Independent Church. Thousands crowded Queen's Park Arena, New Westminster, just up the hill from the churches of Sheepshanks and Sillitoe. And the United Church leaders were there.

Four thousand Anglicans and United Church members came together at the Agrodome for a Unity Meeting. "We all stood and sang the doxology," remembers Archbishop Gower, "and A.B.B. Moore stood there with tears running down his cheeks."

At that twenty-second meeting of General Synod, Principles of Union with the United Church were presented by Godfrey Gower. And the Principles were approved. "We thought," says Archbishop Gower, "we had made a step."

But that late summer week in 1965 was to be the high point in the official relationship between the churches. Although agreement had been reached on major doctrinal differences, progress toward union stalled. Four years later, under the headline "Moving

General Synod met in 1965 in New Westminster. Bishop Gower (left) and Primate Howard Clark (centre) welcomed Jacob Lakdasa de Mel, Metropolitan of India, Pakistan, Burma and Ceylon, and Isabelo de los Reyes, Supreme Bishop of the Philippines, and Camilo Diel, his Bishop.

Michael Ramsey, Archbishop of Canterbury, with Mrs. Ramsey (left) following service in Christ Church on 1966 diocesan visit. The crowd was too large for the Cathedral, but many waited for the Archbishop outside.

towards Day of Decision," Godfrey Gower wrote: "The divisions amongst Christians are a scandal and nothing emasculates the work and witness of the Churches as their ghetto-like denominationalism. The world rightly reminds us that before we offer advice on how to settle its problems we should set our own house in order – 'Physician, heal thyself.'

"This is not to say that denominations of themselves are a sin. Most grew up in history because believing men and women thought some vital truth about the Faith was being ignored. The sin is in perpetuating them and denying the work of God's Holy Spirit, which is always to seek to mend broken unity.

"If we are not interested in healing the divisions in the Church we are party to that dereliction. We may not know how that unity is to express itself in the future. Maybe the Church-to-be would hardly be recognized by us, although one cannot but believe that it will be the vehicle of basic truths about God and man's relation to Him and to themselves.

"For many years now the Anglican Church has been working towards a new expression of unity with the United Church of Canada. We are not interested in a 'merging' of two organizational units. We are interested in an 'emerging' Church—each coming out of itself and taking what is true into a community of Christians, each asking God for charity and discernment to recognize what is true in each other, and each working together to develop a visible Church, recognizable by the world as an expression of its belief, its life and its work."

But union of the kind Moore and Gower had dreamed of was not to happen; not then, anyway. After years had passed, a committee member, the Reverend Dr. D.R. Owen, said, "There is no longer anything that would justify the continuation of the long, expensive and time-consuming efforts to achieve a bilateral organizational union." And in the St. Stephen's, West Vancouver, *Parish News,* the Reverend E.H. Wallace dismissed "this plan of union which we believe to have been spawned in desperation and hatched in expediency. It must have been manifestly clear to the leaders of the two churches for some time now that almost everyone is in favor of this union except the people of the church.

"Surely what is needed today," Wallace continued, "is church unity rather than church union. Why must organic union be forced upon us when we still find it difficult to generate any real feelings of Christian unity?"

It was decided that the two churches would work together in communities, sharing ministry responsibilities in certain areas, but that there would be no union.

"I was deeply hurt," says Archbishop Gower. "I had tried to cultivate, all through my ministry right from the very start, the relationship between the other denominations. There were one or two setbacks, one or two nasty things said to me—but I never let it interfere with me, because I knew that if we don't move together and recognize a common Lord and work for the same purpose, we're not going to make an effective witness.

"A fragmented church is no way to meet the problems of today. And it's all very well to say we can come together if we want to attack a common problem, but there's something more to unity than that—there's a growing together, attaining a spiritual rapport and building up the community of the spirit."

Archbishop Gower talks of theological barriers to the unity of people, and says, "This is the bad conscience of the church. And we'll have to deal with our bad conscience for a long time."

He tells a story of a small band of soldiers during the war, closer to the trenches than their churches at home. "One of them took a tin cup and one of them found a bottle of wine. They scurried around and got some bread. And one said as much of the communion service as he could think of. And they partook of one cup and ate of one piece of bread. The essentials of the unity of the church were right there. All the rest is secondary."

Still—"maybe this is in the providence of God. Maybe it was not the way to bring them together. Maybe we were being told to work together. It may come."

In the late 1960s, the diocese commisioned Price Waterhouse and Company to study its structure and operations and recommend "how the church might best shape its approach to meet the changing needs of...the Lower Mainland." A year later, the diocese received and adopted the Netten Report, named for its principal author.

DIOCESE OF NEW WESTMINSTER — PROPOSED PLAN OF ORGANIZATION

THE DIOCESE

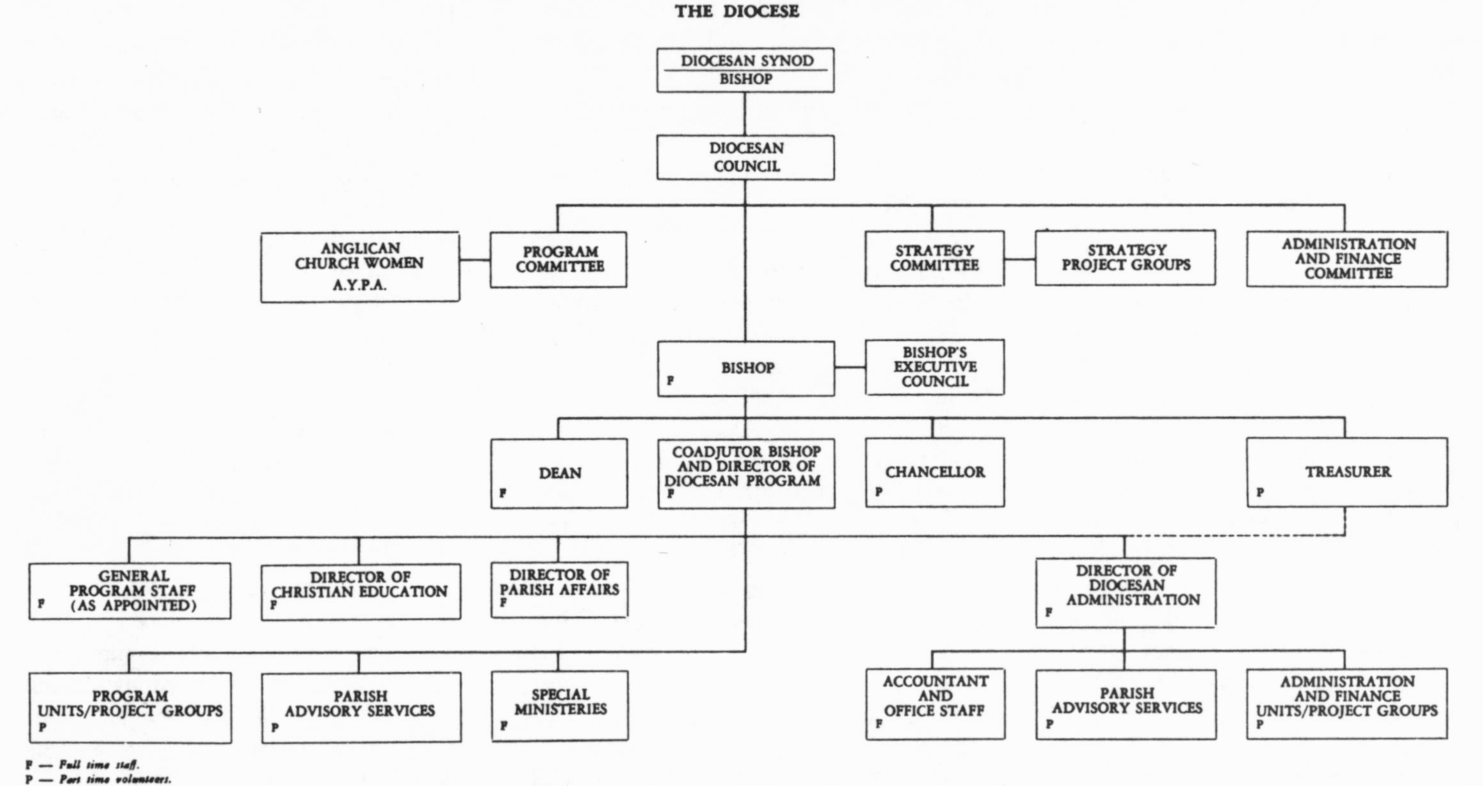

The Netten Report, prepared by Price Waterhouse and Company, was presented to diocesan synod in 1967. It proposed a restructuring of executive responsibilities, and its acceptance led the church nationally towards the development of modern businesslike corporate systems.

The Netten Report recommended changes "intended to improve significantly the effectiveness of the Church in fulfilling its purposes in the complex world of today and tomorrow." The recommendations included episcopal assistance for the bishop (i.e., election of a coadjutor bishop) and appointment of senior diocesan executives to direct program, parish affairs and administration. (The report also suggested a possible future division of the diocese into two or more geographic units, should population growth make that desirable.)

At the sixty-third session of the Synod of the Diocese of New Westminster, Godfrey Gower announced, "This week I celebrated my 68th birthday and I have no intention of saddling the diocese with a decrepit bishop. I would like to retire at the age of 70.... to have some time over the next few years to compose my own soul. I belong to another generation. I want to move over and let someone from the present generation accept responsibility."

Eleven months later at St. John's, Shaughnessy, synod met to elect the diocese's first coadjutor bishop. Twelve priests were nominated, including Archdeacon Watney, Eric Powell, Harold McSherry (who had been a missionary in Hiroshima), Pat Ellis (an early ATC graduate who had worked for the Columbia Coast Mission), N.J. Godkin of St. Catherine's, Henri Taudin-Chabot of St. Chad's and Dean Brian Whitlow of Christ Church Cathedral, Victoria. But the man chosen, in the quickest and clearest episcopal election in diocesan history, was Canon Thomas David Somerville.

David Somerville is entirely a bishop of the Seventies, and a small indication of this is that he has spent the years of his episcopacy living not in an Edwardian see house and not in a third-floor apartment next to the synod offices but at the vertiginous peak of an octagonal high-rise just up from a beach. Here he is able to look out over most of his diocese just as, years ago, he would peer out from the bell tower at St. James's ("like a gargoyle"). He is a Joycean, and this must have had something to do with his choosing Martello Tower for an address. Like Buck Mulligan, he may each morning "bless gravely thrice the tower, the surrounding country and the awakening mountains."

One spring morning in the one-hundredth year of the diocese he leads and the fortieth year of his ministry in it, the bespectacled, rather crane-like Bishop of New Westminster and Metropolitan of British Columbia folded himself into a chair by a window and remembered things.

"I came here in 1929 to go to King George High School. I was living at Salmon Arm, my mother and I, and the high school there was not the very best in the province, so the decision was made to move to Vancouver.

"My mother was Presbyterian, my father was Church of Ireland. He was in the Provincial Police. When she came out to Ashcroft to be married to him, in 1914, one of the first things that had to be arranged was her confirmation.

"I was born in Ashcroft and grew up among the Indian people. There was an old Indian woman called Emily Sisco who maintained stoutly that she was my grandmother. My father died when I was three, in the 'flu epidemic of 1918.

"Canon King at St. Paul's prepared me for confirmation. Archbishop de Pencier confirmed me. And the only thing I remember about my confirmation is that he was wearing a stole (I didn't know it was a stole) with two figures embroidered on it, one on each side, which I could see as I knelt in front of him. I now occasionally wear it to confirmations in the diocese.

"It was while I was at St. Paul's and King George School, towards the end of my time there, that I decided I wanted to be a priest. I had aimed in another direction; I had really wanted to be a doctor, and thought I would go to Normal School and get my teaching certificate and teach for a while to get enough money to do the medical degree – that was in the Depression years and there was no money at all. But I was deflected in another direction, and the thing that deflected me was a mission at St. Paul's that was conducted by Father Cooper of St. James's.

"In all kinds of ways, he was my spiritual father. He taught me how to pray; he heard my first confession; he guided me along while I was going to theological college.

"He preached at St. Paul's during Lent. I went every night to the mission and I was immensely touched by what he said. I went to Canon King and talked to him about the priesthood. He encouraged me and put me in touch with Dr. Vance, who was principal of the Anglican Theological College, and he arranged for me to receive bursary help.

"I didn't enjoy my theological training very much. It was a period when a sort of liberal low church theology was the thing. I was very puzzled by many of the things I was presented with. I went as a raw recruit to the college, went to two lectures, and stayed for lunch, and it was a very inauspicious beginning. One of the lectures was on the New Testament. The lecturer, Dr. Trumpour, explained to us that the Ascension had never really happened, that it was a sort of acted parable. Then I went to a lecture on the Old Testament which was entirely incomprehensible to me. And for lunch we had shepherd's pie with both meat and fish in it, a gathering up of scraps from the whole week. But I managed to survive."

For a while, the Somervilles lived near Vancouver General Hospital. Mrs. Somerville was matron of the internes' home. They were just up the street from Ferguson's Bakery, a neighborhood centre during the Depression for more than one reason. "You could get a weekly bus pass on the streetcars then. Jimmy Ferguson bought a bus pass and all kinds of people used it. You would go into Jimmy's store and get the pass, go downtown, come back and hand it back to him.

"Then my mother went up to Rock Bay, to the Columbia Coast Mission hospital there, to cook. And she went to St. George's School at Lytton, teaching cooking – she was what was called the kitchen matron. I worked one summer at St. George's on the farm. They took on theological students for twenty-five dollars a month and board. One summer I worked at St. Matthew's Church out on East 22nd Avenue. Cyril Stone was then the rector of St. Margaret's and this was one of the parishes he looked after. Another summer, I couldn't find a job anywhere, so I invented one. I went around cutting people's grass and doing gardening. I would go and ring somebody's doorbell and say, 'Your grass obviously needs cutting. I will cut it for you.' A couple of summers, I worked at the college. They kept a student on to cut the grass and be caretaker through the summer.

"You weren't required to be sponsored by a bishop then, so I had no contact with Archbishop de Pencier until he gave the retreat before my deacon's ordination. It was in the little chapel he'd had fitted up in the basement of the old see house on Nanton. Joe Alsop and Tom Bailey were there – three or four of us. The only thing that I can remember was that he told us if we couldn't shine at one end, we ought to shine at the other, and we must always shine our shoes.

"My first job was at St. Mary's, Kerrisdale, with Jim Craig. I was made deacon April 30, 1939. Next year, de Pencier phoned me and told me he wanted me to go to Princeton – B.C., not the university. 'It's not an easy place,' he said, 'but I think you will enjoy it.' I said, 'Yes, my Lord.'"

(He replaced Pat Ellis at Princeton. Forty years later, the handsome, silver-haired Ellis wrote, "We often tell...what failures Margaret and I were when we first went there because we followed Ernie and Weneen Gilbert, and Ernie used to play a hot saxophone at the Saturday night dances and Weneen used to exercise her nursing skills among the parishioners. The pay-off was when Margaret and I were visiting one afternoon and the woman of the house...asked Margaret if she would give her husband an enema.")

"There was no Hope-Princeton Highway," David Somerville continued. "You had to go through Merritt, or you went on the old Kettle Valley Railway. The driving conditions were abominable; there was only one mile of paved road. I inherited an old car from Pat Ellis. It kept breaking down. I found I was working for the local garage rather than the parish. So I went to work nights in the post office. The postmaster was people's warden in the parish. Three nights a week I sorted mail in the post office. The train from Vancouver came at two in the morning and the train from Calgary came at four. So between those periods I would take the little old truck down to the railway station and get the bags of mail. There were always crises."

"I was in Princeton five years. I had Princeton, Hedley, Copper Mountain and Allenby, Nickel Plate, Tulameen and Coalmont. It's fascinating country, that whole Similkameen Valley. I used to take services at the Nickel Plate Mine – in winter I'd go up in the ore bucket.

"Times were really tough at Princeton. The salary was minute and the car allowance

David Somerville (right) and Tom Bailey (later Canon) at Anglican Theological College in 1936.

very small, so every now and then Bishop Heathcote would send me a little gift from his discretionary fund, with a note saying 'I guess this will buy you another tire' or something like that.

"I came back from there in 1945, to Sardis, just outside Chilliwack. And it was like the land of milk and honey. From Sardis I went to St. James's, first as an assistant. St. James's always had three priests, and I came in as number three. That was a sort of golden age for me, because these wonderful old men, Father Cooper and Father Whitehead, both of whom had been there for well over twenty-five years, had had a kind of partnership there, and they had built the place, built the present building. I learned so much from them; such a lot from Father Whitehead, who was the most meticulous and well-organized person I have ever met. And I learned a great deal from Father Cooper, his enormous pastoral care for people and his absolute fearlessness. He'd wade right into the middle of any situation."

(Father Cooper wrote: "David Somerville had always been our friend from his student days....I remember vividly entering Bishop Heathcote's office to consult him about a successor at St. James. 'What do you want?' barked the Bishop. 'My Lord, may I please have David Somerville at St. James?' To that he answered with some force, 'No!' I bowed and said, 'Thank you, my Lord,' and began my exit. Then came the well known voice, 'Here, come back, you old rascal, Cooper. Yes, you can have anything you like, only don't be in a hurry.'" Four years later, Father Cooper asked again, and Heathcote said yes, but to David Somerville he warned, "Don't go. Don't nail your colors to the mast like that. You'll get stuck in that Anglo-Catholic place and you'll never go anywhere.")

"Even then [Cordova and Gore] was a slum area, although a lot of families were living around St. James's. Father Cooper's sister Phyllis organized a thing called the Parish Mothers for women round about, and we used to laugh about it, for many of them were neither mothers nor married, or were mothers and not married."

"It was a place that was full of laughter—great fun, always—a lot of laughing and a lot of hard work and an immense amount of praying."

"Then Father Cooper and his sister left—we put them on the boat—and it was just as if God had left and was going to England. Eddie Hulford and Don Belway and I drove them to New Westminster and said goodbye. And he gave me a parting word of advice. He said, 'David, don't pay any attention to church talk. There'll always be chunterers.' (That's a wonderful old Yorkshire word for people who grumble.) 'They really don't understand,' he said, 'and they're usually on the wrong tack.' After we'd put him on the boat, we were all feeling very low, so we came back to the clergy house and moved furniture.

"I saw him in England many times. He had three sisters, and one of the reasons he wanted to go back was to look after the two who were still there. So he said he had left the clergy house to move into a sisterhood."

Sometimes, Father Somerville would go into the St. James's bell tower. "I was looking over the parish, and reflecting that there were three groups of people who came to the church—the drifters who were down below on skid road, the people who lived in the district, mostly old age pensioners, and the other people who lived all around the lower mainland, on the North Shore and in Burnaby and Shaughnessy. I conceived it as my job to bring these three groups of people into some sort of workable relationship with one another so that they understood each other.

"In the Fifties, there was a mini-depression. Leonard McFerran was with me then, and John Thomas. The town filled up with unemployed single men. It was during the winter and they had come from all over Canada, and they couldn't get relief, because they hadn't been here long enough to qualify. The Sisters down the street had a bread line, and the Salvation Army was doing its best to cope, but the problem was finding somewhere for these men to sleep. So we decided to open the basement of the church. One of the clergy was always there. I took a sleeping bag down, but couldn't sleep because of the horrendous snoring. Tom Alsbury was mayor then, and he was rather sympathetic towards us. He came down to see what was going on, surrounded by reporters and cameramen, and the result was that the city...opened one of the buildings at the PNE and they got beds from the army camp and carried the crisis through.

"Early one morning I'd been out taking the sacrament to a family on Commercial Drive. On the way back, I came to the intersection of Second Avenue where the bridge comes across and, the next thing I knew, I woke up in hospital. I've no idea what happened. I hit another car and then ran into a stone wall. I blacked out completely. I was charged with driving without due care and attention. The police chief then was George Archer, who belonged to St. James's. Eddie Hulford went and appeared on my behalf, and I was fined twenty-five dollars, which George Archer paid.

"It took me a long time to recover. I had had a concussion, and I still have some inner ear problems. I thought it was time for me to leave St. James's. I had been there from '49 to '60, the longest I've ever been anywhere. I felt that my job was done. And I had grown so tired...the strain of St. James's, the continuous pressure of the clergy house, the doorbell and the telephone—there was just no relief. The continuous battering of the needs of the men from roundabout and the relentless pastoral pressure of the place began to get to me. And I thought, I must change, I've got to get away.

"And so, when I heard that Bernard Barrett, who was then dean of residence at ATC, would be leaving, I went to Bishop Gower and said, 'That's the job I want.' And he said, 'Might be a very good idea.'

"I was there five years, as dean of residence and lecturer in pastoral theology. I enjoyed very much the teaching and the work with the students, but I didn't much enjoy the hotel-keeper side of it, or the

Gene Diespecker on mop, Jim Moir on guitar, at ATC in 1960 when Canon Somerville was Dean.

whole undergraduate 'let's go get the engineers' or 'let's go get Union College' sort of thing." (Don Dodman, an ATC alumnus now rector of a suburban Edmonton church, remembers a noisy water fight in the middle of one night. Dean Somerville, padding from his rooms to see what was happening, had a hose thrust into his hands and found himself standing at a window dousing raiders from another college.)

"The theological school always had tremendous crises. Every year there'd be something—a professor would be fired or a student would be refused ordination or they'd have to change the principal. I relied on Godfrey's judgment on a number of things.

"I was travelling around Europe the summer of 1965, and, when I came back, there was a series of telegrams and messages from Toronto saying would I please phone Derwyn Owen, who was then Provost of Trinity They were looking for someone to take over the job as general secretary of the General Board of Religious Education. Michael Creel had been really outstanding as general secretary—he was the one who engineered the new curriculum, he was the one who got Pierre Berton to write *The Comfortable Pew* (they were hoping it would be a Lent book), he was the one who had introduced into the Canadian church the whole small group business, group dynamics. The GBRE was just boiling with ideas and renewal and reform and excitement.

"Michael felt it was time for him to move on. And they (the executive of GBRE) were looking for someone to take over from Michael who would try to damp things down a little bit and yet not blot it all out.

"I had no idea this was what they were looking for. I arrived in Toronto for the interview not really knowing what it was all about, but knowing that I was supposed to follow Michael, and thinking, good heavens, that is really quite an extraordinary thing to do! And I agreed to do so. And then when I got there in September, I discovered that the GBRE staff had not been consulted about this. They were very hostile. I was the unknown, uptight, high church Anglo-Catholic from the Far West who was coming to put the plug in all the wonderful things they were trying to do. They were in shock for three reasons: They mourned Michael's leaving—he was the guru. They were angry because they had not a hand in the choice of

"The election comes as quite a surprise! I...ah... don't know really what to say."—*Anglican Digest.*

his successor. And they were in shock because the New Curriculum had not really reformed the Canadian church. (It was designed, really, to bring a parish to life; it was an attempt to restore education as the centre of parish life, and the curriculum just didn't do this, it was too ambitious.) And the church had not welcomed *The Comfortable Pew* as a blessing. They were hostile about it. So I arrived in Toronto to take over a department in disarray, that felt the church was angry with it and disappointed in it. I tried to minister to them, tried to offer them leadership, but met with a great deal of hostility and misunderstanding. The year as general secretary was a very bad year for me.

"Then the move to reorganize the national office began and I was asked to take a hand in that. One of the features of the reorganization was the putting together of the old empires in new associations—the social service empire, the religious education empire, the missions society empire, a whole lot of them. They were reorganized under Parish Services, National World Services, Communications, and so on. And they said, we really need some person who will be in charge of the lot, and they asked me if I would do that. So my job changed once more and I now had the grand title of Executive Director of Program. And we managed to put the departments together and start working in a new pattern. And then I was elected bishop here.

"I knew that I had been nominated. Tom Norris phoned me—old Judge Norris, he was part of the nominations committee—and he phoned me to ask if I would allow my name to stand. I was pretty sure I wouldn't be elected. But I thought, oh well, it would be rather nice to go back to Vancouver. My mother was still alive then and living here."

"And then I was told by Bill Lowe who had come to work with me—I got Bill to come and join me in Toronto—that the election was going to be on a particular date. Bill came out for the election—he's on leave from this diocese still—and he warned me to stay by the telephone. It was in November of '68, and they phoned me from St. John's, Shaughnessy, where the election was taking place—it was Doug Whitworth who called me—to say I had been elected, I think on the second ballot, and they said, would I accept? and I said yes, I would."

Brother bishops lay hands on David Somerville at his 1969 consecration in the PNE Agrodome.

David Somerville, sixth Bishop of New Westminster, at 1974 confirmation of candidates from St. Helen's and Christ Church Cathedral. In his Easter message, Bishop Somerville wrote: "My prayer is that in Christ you will find renewal of faith, release from anxiety and very great joy."

his successor. And they were in shock because the New Curriculum had not really reformed the Canadian church. (It was designed, really, to bring a parish to life; it was an attempt to restore education as the centre of parish life, and the curriculum just didn't do this, it was too ambitious.) And the church had not welcomed *The Comfortable Pew* as a blessing. They were hostile about it. So I arrived in Toronto to take over a department in disarray, that felt the church was angry with it and disappointed in it. I tried to minister to them, tried to offer them leadership, but met with a great deal of hostility and misunderstanding. The year as general secretary was a very bad year for me.

"Then the move to reorganize the national office began and I was asked to take a hand in that. One of the features of the reorganization was the putting together of the old empires in new associations—the social service empire, the religious education empire, the missions society empire, a whole lot of them. They were reorganized under Parish Services, National World Services, Communications, and so on. And they said, we really need some person who will be in charge of the lot, and they asked me if I would do that. So my job changed once more and I now had the grand title of Executive Director of Program. And we managed to put the departments together and start working in a new pattern. And then I was elected bishop here.

"I knew that I had been nominated. Tom Norris phoned me—old Judge Norris, he was part of the nominations committee—and he phoned me to ask if I would allow my name to stand. I was pretty sure I wouldn't be elected. But I thought, oh well, it would be rather nice to go back to Vancouver. My mother was still alive then and living here."

"And then I was told by Bill Lowe who had come to work with me—I got Bill to come and join me in Toronto—that the election was going to be on a particular date. Bill came out for the election—he's on leave from this diocese still—and he warned me to stay by the telephone. It was in November of '68, and they phoned me from St. John's, Shaughnessy, where the election was taking place—it was Doug Whitworth who called me—to say I had been elected, I think on the second ballot, and they said, would I accept? and I said yes, I would."

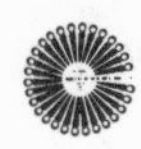

Brother bishops lay hands on David Somerville at his 1969 consecration in the PNE Agrodome.

David Somerville, sixth Bishop of New Westminster, at 1974 confirmation of candidates from St. Helen's and Christ Church Cathedral. In his Easter message, Bishop Somerville wrote: "My prayer is that in Christ you will find renewal of faith, release from anxiety and very great joy."

"Membership Drop Alarming," said the *Anglican News* in November, 1967. Synod was told that church membership in the Anglican Church of Canada was down by 60,000 persons. The church was beginning to seem irrelevant, if not suspect. "Don't trust anyone over 30" was a slogan of the Sixties. "Jesus had some good ideas," pronounced one of the Beatles (a Liverpool rock group), "but after the apostles came a lot of people who messed it up." New York composer-conductor Leonard Bernstein said in Vancouver, "Young people, especially, look for mystical experience. Young people go to church and then go outside and can't relate what people do there to what they heard in church." *The Wall Street Journal* found us living near "a chasm of mistrust, anger and frustration."

We were about to enter the Age of Aquarius. An editorial on Vancouver radio station CHQM told the church it must "learn the language of the age....a few weeks ago, 400,000 young people met at Bethel, New York, in what could only be described as a spiritual event induced through music, grass, beads and bare feet."

Rock masses began to be held at Christ Church Cathedral and other churches. (Not

Dr. Donald Coggan, Archbishop of Canterbury, and Mrs. Coggan welcome David Somerville to 1978 Lambeth Conference. Archbishop Somerville celebrated Eucharist on Canada's day to lead worship.

everyone was convinced—one senior cleric declared, "The electric guitar is the devil's instrument." The acoustic guitar, he said, was all right.)

Herbert O'Driscoll wrote a hymn, printed in the combined Anglican-United Church Hymnal, which spoke of heart surgery, revolution, abortion and the Third World. It was to be sung to the tune of *Song of Joy.* One stanza:

When the launching pad is blazing
And the oxygen ignites;
When the dawn is psychedelic
With a million colored lights;
When the mighty engines thunder
And they speak of Power alone;
Grant our future may be Star-led
As we reach for the unknown.

Longtime CBC foreign correspondent Stanley Burke gave up his job reading the National Newscast and travelled the country pleading for help for the people of Biafra, suffering terribly in the Nigerian Civil War. Dean O'Driscoll invited Burke to deliver his message at a Sunday service in Christ Church Cathedral. Several conservative members of the congregation left, incensed by the cathedral's politics and liturgical experimentation (many not to return until British

"...and, of course, we do expect the new organist to operate the strobe lights, guitar amplifiers and psychedelic sound effects."—*Anglican News* captures the spirit of the mid-Sixties.

industrialist Sir Frederick Catherwood came years later, under the aegis of Regent College, to assure a businessman audience that New Testament strictures against mammon were no longer operative. "He assiduously buttered all their prejudices," said the dean.)

The church's point of view on South Africa's policy of apartheid and Canadian investment in that country presented another dichotomy to Anglicans. The Very Reverend ffrench-Beytagh, former Dean of Johannesburg, visited the diocese. "The church," snapped one man at a cathedral forum, "should stop talking about South Africa." But that wasn't the mood of the church then, nor was it to be.

A wedding in the cathedral was disturbed by an anti-Viet Nam war protest group marching down Georgia Street to the U.S. Consulate, chanting, "One, two, three, four/ We don't want your —— war." The Reverend Philip Thatcher told the wedding guests that the shouts were evidence of the fragmenting world they lived in.

Young Canadians were on the road, hitching rides across the country. Hostels were improvised in towns and cities and along the road, many sponsored by churches.

There was as much hostility as hospitality toward the Aquarian nomads. The Gastown riot, with Mayor Tom Campbell's men-in-blue wielding sticks against the hirsute horde, was a definitive confrontation of straights and hippies. But in Burnaby, the Reverend Bob Purdy of Christ the King believed that the separation of men and women travelling together was unnecessarily cruel (Vancouver maintained separate male and female hostels, some distance apart) and opened the church basement to couples. It was mid summer and the parish committee was away, but the vicar's warden concurred with the plan. When the committee returned, it voted to close the hostel, and an angrily divided congregation met in the parish hall to thrash out the issue. Bishop Somerville, brought in to chair the meeting, announced that he was not there to oversee the removal of the rector (some parish members might have liked to see him, and the vicar's warden, out there with their hippie friends, hitching a ride on Highway 401); he did say that the hostel might have met less resistance if a curtain "walls of Jericho" had been raised between men and women, a la *It Happened One Night*. The banished thumb-trippers moved out of the basement and into parishioners' homes.

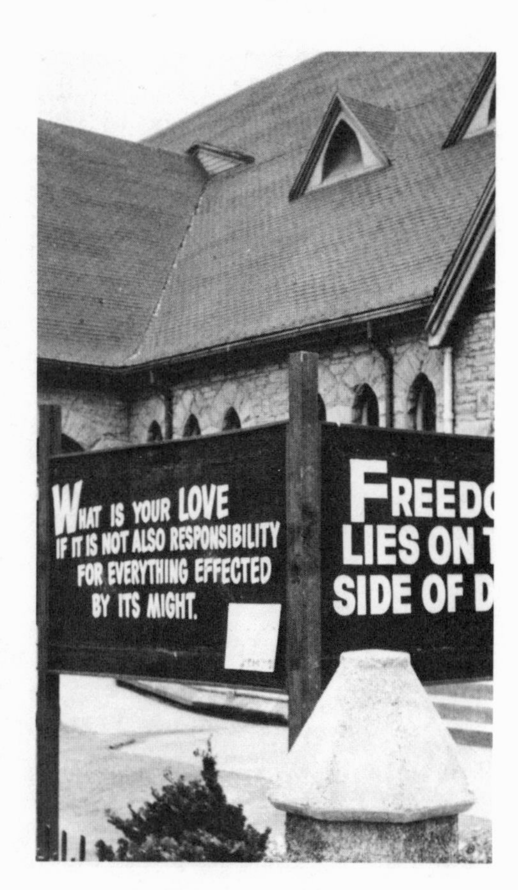

Some Vancouverites objected, but Christ Church offered miniature sidewalk sermons for the Sixties.

A choir of men and boys from Christ Church Cathedral and other diocesan churches, led by Beal Thomas, toured Great Britain in 1966. Here they sing at John Sheepshanks's Norwich Cathedral.

The first Youth Synod was held at St. John's, Shaughnessy, in January, 1969. The delegates endorsed the use of "new media such as films, drama, discussion in small groups, sermons by laity, literature presentations,....as services and sermons are not relevant or meaningful for all people."

FISH, a community "help thy neighbor" movement, began at St. John the Divine, Kingsway, and soon spread to other parishes. Volunteer members were committed to provide help to anyone who called upon them.

Meanwhile, there were spiritual movements developing, none stronger than what was called the "charismatic renewal." Charismatics emphasized the "gifts of the spirit," particularly speaking in tongues. It was, said David Somerville, "the one great lay interchurch movement." People met in each other's homes and in churches. While many Anglican parishes felt the charismatic movement's force, its leadership seemed to come from outside diocesan structures, primarily from the Reverend Robert Birch and members of St. Margaret's Reformed Episcopal Church in East Vancouver.

A less formal style of liturgy began to be popular, lay people helped administer the sacraments, home communions became more

Labor Day work bee at St. Christopher's parish hall, West Vancouver, 1968. Back row, left to right: Janet Stursburg, Tony Fort, Bobbie Wood, Briar Mills, Martha Boyd, Cathy Jukes, Janet Glade, Peg Oram, Harry Boswell and Dianne Oram. Front row: Ginny Boswell and Phyllis Hart.

Travelling religious dramas have been part of the ministry of the Diocesan Youth Unit. *The Rising Son*, Roger Cooper's musical setting of the story of the Resurrection, toured parishes of the diocese in 1978. Larry Jacobs plays the guitar in this scene with the fishermen-apostles.

common. New, less poetic translations of the scriptures were not universally popular ("Like finding a parking lot where a great church once stood," said American essayist Dwight Macdonald), but numbers of people, especially young families, began to discover a place within the church that spoke directly to their circumstances and experiences. For many, the turn-around point came at Sorrento Centre, the lay training camp on Shuswap Lake, where a visitor might find a tee-shirted Ted Scott washing dishes. "Sorrento," said Herbert O'Driscoll, "was a kind of island of the future, where many people who would otherwise have been alienated were enabled to hang in."

Shared communion with other churches was approved by the national Anglican Church; the Diocese of New Westminster began to permit baptized children to receive communion; a service celebrating a diocesan Year of Renewal filled the Agrodome.

There were encouraging signs of ecumenism working in parish situations and in social service projects. Denominations worked out programs of joint ministry and shared church buildings. Church groups found government bureaus more willing to listen to them when they made joint presentations. The Pastoral Institute of British Columbia was formed by United, Anglican, Baptist, Roman Catholic, Lutheran and Presbyterian Churches. Archbishops Somerville and James Carney of the Roman Catholic Archdiocese of Vancouver once found themselves taking tea together with a visiting Tibetan Lama. Most dramatic, however, was the creation of the Vancouver School of Theology, formed by the merger of the Anglican Theological College and the United Church's Union College.

Vancouver School of Theology (VST), founded in 1971, shared a common curriculum, faculty and governing board, along with common ownership of property and endowments. Six years later, VST students included not only members of the Anglican and United Churches, but Baptists, Roman Catholics, Presbyterians and members of the Salvation Army, the Missionary Church and the Church of the Nazarene. Some Anglicans complained ("We don't have a college any more," said one), but VST principal Dr. James Martin, a former faculty member at Princeton and Union Theological Seminaries, said, "An ecumenical school may have this advantage: it is pluralistic. It is heterogeneous, and that reflects the reality of the world."

"Concrete Glass Towers Subordinating Our Lives."

This headline, appearing in the diocesan newspaper *Topic* in January, 1969, introduced an editorial which may have led, in a total reversal of its intention, to the great civic, diocesan and parochial *cause célèbre* of the period: the proposed redevelopment of Christ Church Cathedral.

The editorial was written by the Reverend Grant Dale. He wrote: "It has been frequently suggested that the Church has no right to retain its downtown properties when 'better' use could be made of the land, namely, perch the church in a highrise.... It sounds to me more like a heavy concession to materialism."

To that point, no one had publicly suggested that the cathedral property be redeveloped; but Mr. Dale's column drew an immediate response from the Reverend Ian Grant, then the dean's vicar. "Contrary to Mr. Dale's opinion," wrote Mr. Grant, "I very much believe that 'better' use could be made of the land upon which our many downtown churches stand, especially the land upon which our own Cathedral stands, and I believe that the incorporation of a

Arthur Erickson's design for a tower encasing a cathedral, Christ Church as it might have looked.

contemporary cathedral into a highrise could contribute immeasurably to the humanization of the city....It could make the church more than ever a part of the city [with] a downtown ministry among... thousands upon thousands of human beings."

The next issue of *Topic* brought into the developing battle one of its most dedicated combatants, Mr. Hugh Crisp Fuller, who signed himself "Civil Servant, Law Courts, Vancouver." His letter was headlined "I don't dig you, Mr. Grant." In it, he asked, "Why does Mr. Grant want to change our Cathedral?" and then provided an answer: "It's obviously dollars he's after!"

At this point, the argument began to be given serious consideration; which shows, perhaps, what happens if you let something be talked about too long. Ralph Carder, an influential cathedral member, wrote: "The Reverend Ian Grant's suggestion of combining Christ Church Cathedral in a highrise came as a shock at first and then I thought, why not? and later, as with most brilliant ideas, why hadn't anyone thought of this before?"

The daring idea was loose. Soon both a plan and a rationale for cathedral redevelopment were presented. "Controversy flares," cried the *Topic* headline.

Arthur Erickson was commissioned to design an office tower in which a new cathedral would be incorporated. Dean Herbert O'Driscoll said, "I see possible a mall or rotunda of human resources, a kind of marketplace, not of trading, but of offering." *Topic* reported that the cathedral had suffered a loss of about $20,000 a year for the past three years, a loss which, "if continued would bring the cathedral to a financial standstill within five years. The financial argument," the newspaper continued, "is the most readily understood argument for a new cathedral and office tower complex, as it has been shown that such an arrangement could result in a cash flow to the cathedral of $100,000–$150,000, a fair amount of which would go to the diocese." The site was then valued at $2 million. As for preserving the "Old Root House," its structural life was doubtful anyway; it was, after all, "basically a frame building."

"Eyes of Canadian Church on Christ Church." The article under this April, 1971, headline was written by *Canadian Churchman* editor Hugh McCullum. "A prominent

Calgary clergyman told me," he wrote, "the whole future of inner city parishes—and in almost every city this involves cathedrals—hinges on the outcome of the Vancouver controversy....Herb O'Driscoll and his group of courageous laymen are providing leadership to many of us....We know we have a responsibility to the past, but we also have a responsibility to the future...."

The principle of redevelopment was approved by the cathedral vestry and by diocesan council, and a model was made of the Erickson design. A series of meetings was held with the cathedral congregation, continuing through February, 1972. At the same time, a save-the-cathedral committee began holding meetings; and while there were certainly vocal cathedral members on this committee, the most effective battlers for the 1889 church were non-members—civic officials, architects and politicians.

The Parks Board's George Puil said that he had suggested to the provincial government that the cathedral be declared an historic site, but that if the cathedral were to be demolished, the church should be required to pay the property taxes it had not been charged during the building's existence. Professor Harold Kalman, then a member of the Department of Fine Arts at UBC, said, "Christ Church is indispensable regardless of the merits of a proposed replacement."

"Nice to know they are interested," remarked *Vancouver Sun* columnist Alan Morley. To those pleading for the preservation of the cathedral on the grounds of architectural merit, he declared, "It is strictly late Victorian ecclesiastical cow-barn style, [the work of] a badly confused architect." As for Puil, Morley said, "I have looked carefully through the Thirty-nine Articles...and fail to find any provision in them for the Parks Board to be among the governing bodies of the church."

"There's only one thing wrong with that impassioned slogan, 'Save the Cathedral'," wrote Moira Farrow in the *Sun*. "—it's being shouted by the wrong group. Because it's those who want to knock down the present Christ Church and replace it with a new church who are really trying to save the cathedral."

Grace McCarthy, then Minister without Portfolio in W.A.C. Bennett's provincial government, said that the government would assist in the establishment of a trust fund for the cathedral. *Topic* may have been the first publication to dub Mrs. McCarthy "Amazing Grace." An English authority on cathedrals turned up in Vancouver to assess the debated structure and found nothing much in it to praise, apart from the handsomely carved wooden beams. *En passant,* he gave a poor mark to Holy Rosary, as well. Archbishop Scott, drawn into the argument, said, "The church is not in the business of preserving buildings. It is in the business of forming communities of human resources."

Bishop Somerville sent a letter in June, 1972, to be read in the churches of the diocese. "The real issue," he told them, "is the creation of a new basis for ministry and a new relationship between church community and business community in the centre of the city....We do not feel we have sacrificed spiritual values....Above the Georgia and Burrard corner at the heart of this city will stand a Cross." The bishop got some letters in reply. One said that, under his red robe, he was "Satan himself." Another correspondent regularly sent real estate advertisements, suggesting that the bishop was in the wrong line of work.

On February 6, 1973, the battle ended. Vancouver City Council approved a motion requesting the provincial government to designate Christ Church Cathedral an "historic site." The building had been declared sacrosanct by a vote of eight to three. Dean

The first ordination of women priests in the Diocese of New Westminster, St. Andrew's Day, 1976. Archbishop Somerville leads the recession, including Archbishop Gower and new priests Elspeth Alley (left) and Virginia Briant (right) down the aisle of Christ Church Cathedral.

O'Driscoll called the decision a "failure of imagination" and moved on to other things. The cathedral declined to display the blue Heritage Site plaque on the church building.

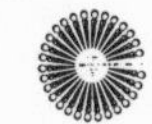

"The place of women in the church has varied from time to time." The speaker is Dr. Hilda Hellaby, first Canadian woman to earn a licentiate of theology from an Anglican college, first Canadian woman to earn a doctorate in divinity.

In 1928, Canon Charles E. Raven of Liverpool wrote *Women and Holy Orders,* declaring, "the admission of women to Holy Orders on an equality with men is inherent in the teachings of Jesus and necessitated by a true understanding of the nature of the Church...it is a matter of theological principle, even more than of justice and expediency."

It took almost half a century for it to happen. On St. Andrew's Day, 1976, women were ordained as priests in the dioceses of Cariboo, Niagara, Huron and New Westminster.

"Do you think that you are truly called," Archbishop David Somerville inquired, "according to the will of our Lord Jesus Christ, and the due order of this Church, to the Ministry of the Church?" Virginia Briant, a one-time Ketchikan collection agent, and Elspeth Alley, a musician who had planned a career as an orchestrater, each replied "I think so."

The conviction that the ordination of women as priests was meet and right had been growing throughout the Canadian church, but the historic events of that St. Andrew's Day were, to a degree, a victory for the Diocese of New Westminster, Archbishop Somerville had been chairman of the Committee on Ministry which presented the resolution on women's ordination to the 1973 General Synod; and Dr. W.R.K. Crockett, VST Professor of Systematic Theology, presented a paper which outlined the theological issues involved and supported the resolution.

The decision to seek ordination had come to both Virginia Briant and Elspeth Alley as a kind of divine surprise. But, said Mrs. Briant, "I knew I had arrived at the time and place where God has wanted me all these years." And Mrs. Alley said, "It wasn't for me to say. It was for God to say."

The ordination of women to the priesthood was not unopposed; one priest, Father James Penrice, rose during the Christ Church Cathedral ceremony to present a formal statement of opposition, and male clergy

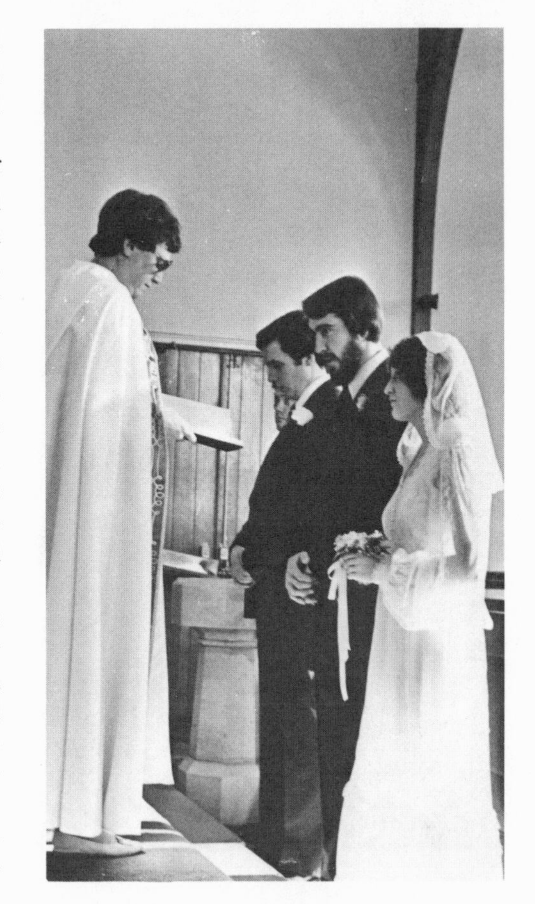

Elspeth Alley, one of Canada's first woman priests, officiates at the marriage of her daughter.

Ralph Dean, executive secretary of the Anglican Communion, was acting principal of ATC 1959-60.

have the option of not recognizing the authority of their sister priests. One priest, Father Edward Gale, formed the Parish of St. Mary and St. Martha as part of the Anglican Catholic Church, a group of North American Anglicans who, dismayed by liberal tendencies within the church, including the ordination of women, have separated from it. But now, for most, woman as priest is an accepted reality. Like other movements of the Sixties and Seventies, it has, in Herbert O'Driscoll's words, "passed through its first great burst and settled into a quiet and stable methodology."

In the late summer of 1969, the Right Reverend Ralph Dean, executive officer of the Anglican Communion, stunned delegates to General Synod in Sudbury. Dean—on leave from the Diocese of Cariboo—had spent five years travelling the world and was appalled by its inequities and furious at the affluent North American church's ignorance and indifference. In a blistering jeremiad, he warned Canadian Anglicans that in ten years time the church as it was then known would have ceased to exist. "We'll have to become the pilgrim church, much smaller, but bearing more of the marks of the body of Christ."

"We possess all things," he said. "That's why we have nothing." He told delegates that Canadian Anglicans were living a criminal life in the standard of living they had accepted. "Until we adhere to a style of life that even begins to look like Christian, then the world is not going to hear us."

"I believe, within my lifetime, that we will be the church of the dispossessed. We'll have to die if it is to live."

In *Canadian Churchman,* Bishop Dean said the church often could not speak meaningfully to the world because "its voice is frequently just an echo of the world itself." He urged the church to stop being "club-like" and become "ruthlessly radical."

But, he explained, "radical," in its primary sense, means "going to the roots." "It is to our roots," said Ralph Dean, "that we must look. It is to Christ...."

Six months later, the Diocese of New Westminster approved a resolution that first priority and a definite financial commitment be given to local and world relief and development. And a year after that, the national church chose as its leader a man who had grown up in East End Vancouver during the Depression and had a tough-jawed commitment to social action: Edward Walter "Ted" Scott.

"There's a lot of injustice in the world," said the new Primate, "and this can destroy you completely unless you can live creatively in the midst of it."

Soon, social action was the most visible part of the church's program, and its foci were the Primate's World Relief and Development Fund and local and national Public Social Responsibility Units. Ted Scott was, wrote Kenneth and Barabara Bagnell in *The Canadian,* "the most influential figure in Canadian religion." He was also the most effective burr under the saddle of Canadian business, especially when the Anglican Church ceased to be a passive investor in corporations with international dealings and began using its power to influence corporate policy.

"It used to be that the churches in Canada preoccupied themselves with telling people about God," complained the *Vancouver Province* in 1977. "Apparently that's no longer the case. Nowadays, you'll as likely find clergy...cluttering the boardrooms of the nation and shareholders' meetings, railing and harassing business executives on the corporate sins of multinational corporations. An organization calling itself the Taskforce on Churches and Corporate Responsibility...wants companies ...to cease doing business with countries like Chile and South Africa, because they have oppressive regimes."

"Not content with dictating to the business community its moral obligations," the editorial went on, "Anglican and Roman Catholic Churches set up Project North to keep business out of Canada's northern reaches. Some of their views shaped the thinking of Mr. Justice Berger."

The ruling class has never liked prophets much – it prefers priests who know their place – but the surprise was that many Anglicans were sympathetic to business and government and angry at their church. Less than ten years after New Westminster synod passed the relief and development resolution and another motion requiring "research into social and political issues, with...suggestions for church action," it had to deal with resolutions seeking to limit such activity. Of particular concern to many was the Anglican Church's contributions to the World Council of Churches (moderator of the WCC central committee: Ted Scott) which continued to provide funds to African liberation movements. So far, the Primate's view of social responsibility has continued to be supported by a majority of the church, despite growing conservative resistance.

"I think what we've begun to recognize more and more," says Ted Scott, "is that so many of the decisions of our society are not individual decisions, but are made by corporate bodies. We need to be concerned about corporate decisions, about government policy, as well as about the needs of individual people. It isn't either/or, it's both/and.

"It's always been a problem to me," he explains, "how you can talk about loving your neighbor, loving people, without being concerned about the kind of impact that the conditions they live under have upon them."

Archbishop Scott has travelled the country, discussing the church's policies with parish, diocesan and business groups. In 1977 he wrote to *The Financial Post:* "The focus of action is not to create victims but to seek to get groups to examine, and perhaps decide to change, behavior. If a government, business concern, or any other corporate institution (including the church)

Archdeacon Charles Wilkins, director of parish affairs, at 1973 Clergy Conference in Manning Park. Bearded man behind him is the Rev. Lance Stephens, an ex-Simoon Sound logger.

can change its behavior so that people can be treated more humanly, as beings loved by God, in the Canadian North, in Africa, in urban communities or anywhere in the world, this is the desired result." And, he concluded, "Many individuals and a number of institutions do not see themselves as 'targets' but as willing associates in such an enterprise."

The following spring, standing in his Indian beaded robes in the pulpit of East Vancouver's St. Thomas's Church, the Primate said, "We live in a world full of divisions. The calling of the Christian church in that world is to bear witness to a new kind of community—a unity beyond our ability to express.

"One of the ways it is given us to love God is to love those whom God loves."

In 1975, the diocese released the reports of two study groups: the Task Force on the State of the Church and the Task Force on the Environment. The state of the church had changed markedly from what it was when Acton Sillitoe arrived. The diocesan boundaries had shrunk (they were now Hope and Powell River rather than Fort Steele and Nechako), parishes had grown from a handful to eighty, and diocesan clergy and staff numbered considerably more than the four who welcomed the Sillitoes at the New Westminster wharf.

There had been other changes. The number of worshippers that year was 41,621, a drop from 64,446 in 1970. Diocesan receipts were up, to $574,487, reflecting an increase in per capita giving, and more than a third of the diocesan budget was being spent for work internationally and in the far North. Seventy-three per cent of parishes were involved in social service outside their own membership, 71 per cent were providing financial aid outside parish boundaries, and 55 per cent were participating in ecumenical activities.

The report cited "the great diversity which exists from parish to parish suggesting the impossibility of complete uniformity of

Two towering laymen of the mid-twentieth century: longtime treasurer Peter Kaye and committee man Cyril Hodge. The veteran delegates are seen at 1976 Synod with Eric Powell.

In the diocese's first century, parish picnics have probably changed less than anything else.

policy. Ours is a diocese," it concluded, "which needs a higher profile for its policies, but which, at the same time, requires those policies to have a sufficient degree of flexibility to enable them to be adapted to some degree to the differing needs of different churches."

"God has given us grace," says David Somerville, "to live together in extraordinary diversity, at the heart of which there is a strong unity. There is great liberty to individual persons within parishes, to parishes within the diocese, and to dioceses within the church. From the outside, it looks like a muddle. But from the inside, it feels like freedom."

The Task Force on the Environment soberly examined the society in which the Diocese of New Westminster is set, and found "one of the most affluent communities in North America, and a setting of natural beauty. Yet beneath the affluence and beauty, people live with many anxieties ....the Vancouver Crisis Centre alone receives 2,200 calls a month...."

The study identified various phenomena evident in the diocese in the mid-1970s, including "Family breakdown...many people seem to find it easier or feel that it is better to let their relationship break apart, than to stay together and work at the issues between them....Increase of crime. . . while many regard present methods of dealing with crime as being unsatisfactory....Management-labor conflict... the two sides have become more ideologically separated...there appears to be little acceptance of a partnership...there is also a growth of hostility...toward the labor movement and a crisis of direction and purpose... within the labor movement itself....Social stratification...with little contact between rich and poor [and] the division of many neighborhoods...according to the cost of housing or ethnic origins...Growing disenchantment with politicians and with the political options available....Sense of powerlessness."

"What are some of the specific things the church can do to make the world more human, more caring?" asked Bishop Somerville. "That's the business we're in. Christ didn't die for the church. He died for the world."

Within the church in the Diocese of New Westminster, there had always been men and women to answer this question. Seven decades before the Task Force's report

that "many regard present methods of dealing with crime as...unsatisfactory," the Reverend C.C. Owen of Christ Church, an executive of the Children's Aid Society, said, "It is perfectly wonderful how much is spent on gaols and penitentiaries and how comparatively little we spend in tracking things back to their causes and trying to prevent the creation of criminals. I feel the principle of prevention is one we cannot emphasize too greatly."

At Oakalla Prison, a 1968 workshop organized by Father Hulford brought more than one hundred clergy, laity and corrections officials together to consider alternatives to the present criminal justice system. They heard Ted Harrison, Regional Director of Corrections, speak against class bias in Canadian law. And he told them, "Crime evolves out of the community and it's up to the community to stop it."

A familiar figure in Vancouver courts is Eric Powell, diocesan director of program, a priest and social worker who has worked at Haney Correctional Institute. "This is an area," he says, "where the church has to become more involved. If you're managing and controlling people, you do that through legislation and laws, so one of the most

Eric Powell visits Anglican Theological College alumnus Cornelius Olowemeye (later Archbishop Olowemeye) and his family in Ondo-Benin, Nigeria. Powell is now Diocesan Director of Program.

Rozalia Boda, director of the crafts program at the Gastown Workshop, with rug-maker Anton Sarkozy. The St. James's social service project lets people be "a family helping one another."

powerful groups in society is not the church and clergy, it's courts and lawyers. Often lawyers are the 'spiritual directors' of the new society–I wonder, do they accept that responsibility?

"The church has a very important role in talking about the meaning of justice. The church still stands for the longing and the yearning of man to do what is good. [Its job is] to remind growing bureaucracies of sensitivity and caring, to remind the government the city is more than buildings. Vanier speaks of 'the broken people.' The church's role in caring for the broken is so real in big cities."

In *I Heard the Owl Call My Name,* the bishop says, "The church belongs in the gutter. It is where it does some of its best work." The words echo Godfrey Gower's voice and Eric Powell's ministry. Either might have said it.

In the core of Vancouver, St. James's Social Service Society continues to care for the broken people. A group called the Downtown Clergy, twelve men and May Gutteridge, went to City Hall and got support for skid road projects. Mrs. Gutteridge and three women from other churches began working with alcoholics. Then they started making sandwiches and soup ("it was all very illegal, but the inspectors were very good"), which led to a cafeteria now serving a thousand meals a week. A clinic was opened, to provide "medical help quickly, without always having to go and beg of it." Denominational tags disappeared. The Anglicans used detoxification equipment provided for The Pilot, a United Church project, backed by a group of Presbyterian businessmen. They worked in a Roman Catholic building and a Jewish doctor donated his time.

The skid road group got support from the Vancouver Welfare Department, the Junior League, Dr. Al Connolly of the Drug Commission, columnist Jack Wasserman, broadcaster Jack Webster, lawyer Mary Southin, journalist-politician Simma Holt, writer-broadcaster Chuck Davis, Dr. Helmut Ruebsaat, Dr. Howard, Minister of Human Resources Bill Vander Zalm, the Canada Works Program, Anglican Church Women, New Horizons, LIP and RAP, St. Faith's and other parishes, always St. James's, and its Cordova Street Roman Catholic neighbor, St. Paul's.

The Pensioners' Club started serving hot meals to its elderly members. The Gastown Workshop program began with brick-making, carpentry, painting, upholstery work, a furniture store, a weaving centre, an electrical repair shop, a thrift shop ("We are teaching these people how to live in society, how to be useful members, how to be a family helping one another," says May Gutteridge). Victory Hotel was bought for the program by the city—it's now called Victory House. The society gives away furniture, clothing, meals; takes food to the sick, moves furniture for people who can't afford transportation, maintains a home help program. Many of the young women who have been trained by the society are now earning salaries in full-time clerical jobs. "We have seen many people get on their feet and go off and develop their own lives," says Mrs. Gutteridge. There are community weddings—community funerals. "The people...know they will be looked after."

But despite all this success, the East End workers find that life on skid road hasn't gotten better since society first learned of *The Ecstasy of Rita Joe.* "Problems are much more extreme than in the Sixties," says May Gutteridge. "It's a very sad situation. The quality of life for many is one of the disgraces of our civilization."

Above the Gastown Workshop is Powell Place, part of May Gutteridge's St. James's Social Service.

Sarah and Ray Walker, directors of 1970s hostel for battered wives and children, maintained by the parish of St. John the Evangelist, North Vancouver, under Rector Fred Thirkell.

Powell Place is the new hostel for women and children in the area. It opened in April, 1977, and in its first two years sheltered 870 women and 189 children. Monica Hogg wrote this report from Powell Place:

"Shortly after we opened, we took in a classically beautiful native woman who had left her boyfriend after a severe beating. She had a serious drinking problem, and, while sober, was painfully shy. During her first visit, she rarely made eye contact with any of us. Her eyes never left the floor. She had a good sense of humor, despite an intense sadness, behind all that thick black hair that hung over her face. She let me read some poetry that she had written and I was impressed by her intelligence. She read voraciously and did crossword puzzles.

"At nine years of age she had been placed in a foster home. She became very close to the family she stayed with. After several years, she was moved to another foster home. She ran away, back to the family she loved. They made it very clear to her that they did not want her anymore. The list of foster homes grew. She never knew love of any kind. When she came of age, she left the foster homes and became involved with men who drank heavily and abused her physically and verbally. She had two children. Both were taken away from her.

"After leaving us, she stayed with a family for a while and went to school, but this did not work out. She later got involved with Alcoholics Anonymous and met a man there. They started drinking together. He beat her. On one occasion he took a knife to her and forced her to humiliate herself in front of a group. She would leave him for a while, but he would find her and tell her how he loved her and she would return to him. They would drink their welfare money and it would be gone. They ate in sandwich lines and at missions. By this time she was pregnant.

"All through her pregnancy she lived in hotels on Hastings Street, eating any free food available. One night in a bar, she broke a beer glass on the table and used the jagged stem to slash her swollen belly. Another night her boyfriend got into a fight with some people on the street...later that night they came after her and beat her in revenge.

"She and her boyfriend decided to start a new life and left Vancouver. A beautiful boy was born[to them]. After a time they were drinking. He began to beat her and she ran away. The next day she went to Welfare and asked for their assistance to get the child away from him and for money to live on.

Canon Stanley Higgs, veteran chaplain, social service worker and Central City Mission director, with Haney Correctional Institute inmate and the painting executed by the artist-prisoner.

Timothy Nakayama, rector of St. Peter's, Seattle, and his mother, the former Lois Masui Yao, a 1920s Church of the Ascension kindergarten teacher, at the 75th anniversary of Holy Cross Church.

John Jeffries, the priest in charge of the New Westminster Diocese's urban ministry to Indians.

He had already been there...they believed him over her painfully hesitant, shy plea. She was given four dollars and a twenty-five dollar food voucher. She landed in a bar, got drunk and went home with a stranger.

"The next day, hysterical, she called me. I contacted her social worker, a woman who had stuck by her and really cared. She called Welfare in the other city. They didn't find the baby for two weeks and when they did, he was very sick from neglect. He was put in the hospital, then into a foster home, while she stayed at the YWCA. When the baby was well enough, he was returned to her and she flew home to us. The baby was still quite sick and she took good care of him. It was obvious she loved this little creature with all her heart.

"She found an apartment, furnished it and moved in with the child. It was the first time she had lived alone and the first time she had had such an immense responsibility. She started drinking again. She was evicted. On the day she was to move, the movers arrived to an open door, a pile of boxes and a note. She disappeared for a week.

"After finally surfacing, she started going to A.A. again. Her social worker arranged for her to take assertiveness training. She began to see a therapist at a Community Care team, who had been helping her to feel good about herself. She has been sober now for two months.

"The last few times I saw her, she bounced into the room, confident, her head held high, meeting my eyes. I have seen her talking with strangers, looking them directly in the eye. It's a beginning. She is 21 years old."

As the diocese approached its centennial, roots that had been put down decades before flourished. Columbia Coast Mission, now administered jointly by the Anglican and United Churches, was carrying on its work by seaplane as well as ship. The oldest congregation of Chinese Anglicans in Canada, the Church of the Good Shepherd, had become the fastest growing parish in the diocese as new families arrived from Hong Kong. Canon Gordon Nakayama was back in Vancouver, priest of the Japanese community at Holy Cross Church, as Japanese Christians in North America celebrated the Japanese Christian Mission Centennial. The Reverend Timothy Nakayama wrote, "The second war, though it created hardships, enabled the Japanese to know Canada at first hand, and the rest of Canada to know the Japanese Canadians. The Japanese who came to Canada settled largely on the Pacific slope due to economic and geographical factors, few went farther inland. Following the Canadian declaration of war on Japan all Japanese, Canadian-born or otherwise, were forcibly removed from the coastal strip. As a result many of them found new and interesting lives in other parts of Canada....[and] because of the loyalty and devotion of the missionaries and of the Japanese Christians, many were brought to love God and to serve Him in His Church." "The Oriental people," says Eric Powell, "will have a significant influence on this diocese in the next few years."

At the Flying Angel Club, Padre Joe Parker and Missions to Seamen continued to serve twelve thousand sailors a year from more than seventy countries. In 1979, more than half British Columbia's Indian people were living in cities. The Reverend John Jeffries, a North Ontario Cree, came with his Mohawk wife, Jean, to begin an inner city Anglican-United ministry to native people in Vancouver. "It will not be an easy row to hoe," he said, "but we are

Pyramid of warm socks for sailors, knit by Anglican Church Women for Christmas, 1978.

The beloved "Tante"—"the Florence Nightingale of the Vancouver waterfront" for thirty years.

English sailor repaying kindness at Flying Angel Mission works on "around the world" clocks.

excited about the move."

On Gambier Island, 55-year-old Camp Artaban had enlarged its holiday/mission program to include families and single adults, reaching across the socio-economic spectrum. Some Artaban children go to the camp on social aid: some are flown there by private helicopter. Diocesan program units had multiplied to include committees on family life, children's work, native affairs, youth activities, public social responsibility, world relief and development, leadership development, and retreats.

"I'm convinced," says Eric Powell, "that the Seventies and Eighties will put the Diocese of New Westminster in a megalopolis situation. We're going to be one big city from the North Shore to Chilliwack. I sit here and look out over the city—how do you influence the spirituality of this? The church wants to preserve the dignity of people, and the influence of the cross of Christ in the centre of the city. The church has provided the caring, the social services, the counselling and the nurturing of people over the last hundred years. All the welfare systems in the world will not take the place of the caring church. The church is the last bastion of the volunteer society.

"Tiffany at the tiller" is the Rev. Ron Harrison's title for this glimpse of Camp Artaban in the summer of 1978. The 55-year-old Artaban has enlarged its traditional program to include family and singles camps.

Oldest and Youngest campers at Artaban in 1975: Jack Whitworth, 87; Andrea Wilkins, 1½.

Morning Star performs at an ecumenical festival at Kitsilano Beach. The septet from St. Matthias's Church performed for the public at churches, colleges, coffee houses and prison farms.

"I would have liked to have lived," he grins, "as a territorial archdeacon in the days of Sillitoe. In the early days, it was *the* church. It attracted everyone. When I was with the Columbia Coast Mission, some of my happiest moments were taking services in bunkhouses with loggers. You'd have supper with them and then at the end of the meal get up and say, 'I'm Eric Powell, there'll be a service at five and I'd like you all there.' All these tough guys would look around and say, 'Who's he?' Then you'd go from bunkhouse to bunkhouse and say, 'I'm waiting for you.' And they came.

"We were very quiet in the Fifties and Sixties—there was a period of almost barrenness. But an interesting phenomenon has taken place this past Easter and Christmas: our churches have been full, overflowing. There seems to be a new growth of young families appearing in the churches. The messiah of materialism of the Fifties never really achieved the hopes and aspirations of people, and there is a new spirituality.

"There's an excitement, a tension. Either you move with it or you die. And I don't think we're going to die. We're prepared for the future church."

More than 6,000 Anglicans, including 100 red-robed priests and 250 choristers, attended a service at the PNE Agrodome to begin the 1974-75 Year of Renewal in the diocese.

Parishes of the diocese created individual banners for Renewal service procession at Agrodome.

In 1975, David Somerville was elected Metropolitan of British Columbia at a Council of Provincial Synod at the Cenacle Retreat House. In 1977, he announced his decision to retire in 1980, and his hope that the diocese would elect a coadjutor bishop.

"A Proposal for the Process of Electing the VII Bishop of New Westminster" was presented to diocesan synod in May, 1978, by the strategy committee. One delegate worried that there might be heavy politicking by potential episcopal candidates. Archbishop Somerville said, "The job's not all that attractive."

Many of the men who had held the job had felt that way–Sillitoe might have remained a confidant of royalty, Dart might have stayed in academe, Heathcote could have retired to his baronial castle–but they had been part of what Godfrey Gower calls "a romance, the pursuit of an ideal, the search for the Holy Grail."

"They were tall men, sun-crowned, who lived above the fog in public duty and private thinking." Archbishop Gower was thinking then of the first to come, men like Hills and Sheepshanks. But he might have been describing all six men named New Westminster.

The missionaries had come to "a rough country with no social structure whatever... and given us a picture of what the church does to society. It adds grace, it refines." They came, carrying the truth in front of them, and in search of the truth, and letting the truth work through them, in the face of what Rexroth calls the Great Social Lie. "The church was born and bred in a thorn bush," says Godfrey Gower. "Everything is baptized by the knowledge of the life of Christ."

These early comers (and later ones, too) had no illusions of invulnerable goodness. At his enthronement in 1895, John Dart addressed synod, taking as his text Romans 7:21: "I find then a law, that, when I would do good, evil is present with me."

"The Bishop first dwelt," reported *The Weekly News Advertiser,* "upon the constant conflict between the spiritual or regenerate and the carnal or corrupt nature....The defects of good men and their mistakes should not surprise others or shake their faith. Hardly one of the Old Testament characters, who, on the whole, served God faithfully, was free from glaring fault or crime. So, too, in the lives of those mentioned in the New Testament, could be seen

Priests of the diocese at Year of Renewal service. "Open your eyes to the Lord, the Spirit," said Bishop Somerville. "We are all together members of one another to do God's purpose. I call you to renewal, to be the people of God in the place where God has put you."

Year of Renewal Eucharist con-celebrants at the Agrodome included (from left) Eric Powell, Bill Stephens, Ed Wilkins, Hubert Butcher, Archdeacon Wilkins, Bishop Somerville, Dean O'Driscoll, John Clark, Bob Wild, Ernie Eldridge, David Hawkins, Ray Murrin and Lance Stephens.

religious principles working in the weakness of human nature. Yet despite the blemishes which stained their lives, their sincerity is undoubted. Religious history is very different to what men often wish it to be."

The roots of the diocese and its work are elsewhere, often unknown. "There was a church near us," says May Gutteridge, remembering her childhood in the south of England. "A big church, very similar to St. James's. And I was taken to church at two weeks old and baptized. The church was my life. It was just around the corner and I grew up in it. And there was a wonderful woman called Mary Hunt and she was the parish worker. I don't remember her, but she was a tremendous person. She died when I was little, but she left me a book, a beautiful old book, her Bible, and a picture of herself which I have on my dressing table. And it was the influence of this person that gave me this wonderful gift....I've never wanted to leave the worship of the church. And that's why the name 'parish worker' is to me the greatest honor. Everything we've done here, that's where it started."

"New Westminster is the only diocese in Canada that has moved to license clergy to the bishop of the diocese rather than to a parish," says Archbishop Scott. "I think there are some real strengths in that, in terms of facilitating mobility of clergy, and getting a sense of the diocese and the whole urban community. Because many of the problems of the urban community cannot be worked at by a single parish. There needs to be a diocesan policy in relationship to the metropolitan community, and I think that developments in New Westminster have helped that field of work.

"I think we haven't yet gone far enough in focusing the kinds of specialized ministries we need—not to take the place of, but to go alongside the parochial ministries.... It would be good to have someone—and Eric Powell does this partly now, in terms of the prison situation—to have contact with city council and the government in terms of the church being able to know what policies are being formed and to have some input into those policies and to interpret and help people share more actively in the life of the community. I don't think we're doing enough of that in any place in the country yet."

"We think of those men as giants," says Herbert O'Driscoll of the first priests in the diocese. "The wilderness was a challenging place. But in the city, the challenge is different and requires very different survival techniques.

"We are at the end of a very long era. The church has moved from underground, to dominance over society, through the Renaissance, Reformation, the age of scientific experimentation, Darwin-Freud-Marx, and the moral bombs of two world wars. The church was a majority institution in Western society from the Third Century. We have been to the funeral of all that. We're being asked to live in a new situation.

"Our task is how to live creatively and with integrity when you're borne between the tides—hearing the sad lapping of the old and the thunder of the new.

"A lot has happened in this diocese that didn't happen in other dioceses or that happened only with great difficulty. Now, the forest has been cleared—but there are other forests. Forests of the mind.

"The City of Man is always rising and falling like the landscapes in H.G. Wells's time travels—but the choice is to be a builder of the City of God, which is being built always in the dying City of Man. And that's what makes sense of your life and mine."

Boy choristers of St. John's, Shaughnessy, performed in England in the summer of 1978. Choirmaster and organist Frederick Carter is at centre, back row. The boy choristers were accompanied on the tour by the adult Gallery Singers, who were awarded first place at the Middlesborough Inter-Tie Festival.

"I see the diocese," says David Somerville, "as a place where it's possible to experiment. Partly because of the newness of the city, and the climate—we're the California of Canada, to some extent—I say privately to my friends in the East that people out here don't take the church that seriously anyway. So that it is possible to try things, it's possible to experiment. I know there are people in Eastern dioceses who say, 'What are those crazy fools out on the coast doing now?' and if I hear that, I say, 'Watch out, because before long, it will have reached you.'"

At Sorrento, Archbishop Somerville spoke about the church in the 1980s and offered "four clues to where we're going:

"One: a renewed sense of the mysterious. Disenchantment can only go so far.

"Two: an interest in playfulness. At the very heart of human existence, there is something non-rational, something that makes us laugh, liberates us and stretches us.

"Three: an interest in outer space. For centuries, we have limited our view of God to what has happened on this earth. Now, the most significant poster has changed from the menacing mushroom-shaped cloud to the view of our world from space.

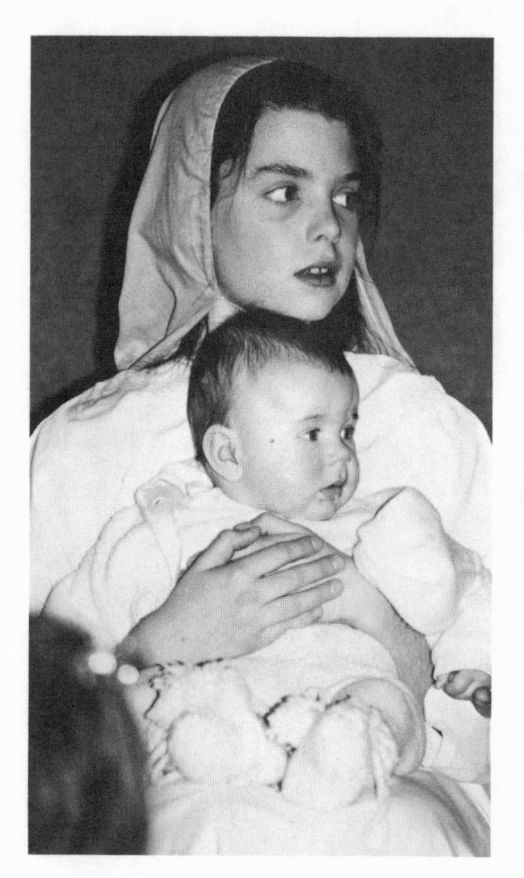

St. Augustine's Christmas pageant, 1978. Jill Farrar plays Mary; baby is her cousin Matthew.

Among his "clues to where we're going," David Somerville includes "an interest in playfulness."

All-night Skatathon in 1979 raised funds for Camp Artaban hut construction. Sixty-nine skaters included several priests who gamely arrived to lead services the following morning.

"Four: interrelations between Eastern and Western cultures. In some scales of Eastern music, there are sixty-four steps from C to C, and Eastern ears that can hear and identify those steps. We can't. But as the world gets smaller, we are brought closer and closer to Eastern insight, its sense of mystery, its sense of reincarnation, and its view of the person as a series of envelopes enclosed one inside another."

September 18, 1893. Acton Windeyer Sillitoe, Lord Bishop of New Westminster, rises at the service of thanksgiving following the first General Synod of the Anglican Church of Canada. These are his words:

"While we rejoice in the unity wherewith God has blessed us, let us never forget that it is not we only that are to be one, but that all are to be one, according to His will. This is our mission, and we may not be satisfied so long as it is unattained. All that we have done is not enough, so long as God has more for us to do.

"We have touched the outer circle of rganic unity amongst ourselves. We have lrawn a circumference of united action. At the centre is God, the Father, Son, and Holy Ghost. At the centre only is perfect unity. There alone is our end; there only is the full accomplishment.

"Now towards this centre must every diocese converge, and every Churchman in every diocese, each one a separate ray, sparkling and bright with holy endeavour and unselfish aim, hastening on by the attractive power of the indwelling Spirit, until all shall be absorbed in the eternal being of God, and He shall be all in all."

'he Rev. John Paetkau greets parishioners at the dedication of the diocese's youngest church: t. Andrew's, Pender Harbor, at Madeira Park on Sechelt Peninsula, consecrated May 17, 1979.

The Rev. Cyril Williams of the Anglican Archives, Vancouver School of Theology, as pictured in *Via Media*, 1960-61. Canon Williams's generously shared knowledge of diocesan history facilitated the editor's research.

Acknowledgements and an Apologia

Given the impossibility of recording with absolute accuracy the activities (their motives, their effects) of a single individual over twenty-four hours, it is inevitable that an account of a century's events, involving thousands of persons, will be found deficient. All through the preparation of this book, I have been haunted by the premonition of readers saying, "But how could you *possibly* leave out dear Reverend So-and-So?" And, alas, they will be right. How could I?

On the other hand, how could I get him, and all the others, in, without running the narrative into fourteen volumes? So what I offer, cap in hand, is a story in which a few have been selected to represent the many.

This is not a conventional history. But perhaps it will help to stir an interest in our ecclesiastical roots. Archbishop Gower said to me, speaking about Bishop Sillitoe, "I love that man!" And now, so do I. And Dart and Heathcote and all the rest. They are not figures of the past; they are alive all

through the diocese, and their stories deserve to be freed from church archives. Maybe this book can be used to prop open the door.

For assistance in the preparation of this book, I thank His Grace, the Archbishop of Canterbury, the Trustees of Lambeth Palace Library and Librarian E.G.W. Bill; Archbishop Edward Scott, Archbishop David Somerville and Archbishop Godfrey P. Gower; Reverend Eric Powell; the Diocesan Centennial Committee, Chairman Conrad Guelke, Secretary Dorothy Miller and Treasurer Tudor Ommanney; publisher Peter Zebroff; the Vancouver School of Theology Archives and Archivist Canon Cyril Williams; *Anglican News, Topic,* and Reverend Ron Harrison; the Anglican Church of Canada Archives, General Synod Archivist Marion Beyea and Assistant Archivist Margaret Millman; the City of Vancouver Archives and Archivist Sue M. Baptie; the Province of British Columbia Archives and Archivist Kent Haworth; the Vancouver Public Library, Mr. Ron D'Altroy, Ms. J. Stephens, and the Department of History and Geography; the New Westminster Public Library; the Burnaby Public Library, McGill Branch; Dean Herbert O'Driscoll and the library and office of Christ Church Cathedral; and Ian Alexander, Arthur I. Andrews, Amy Barker, Reverend John Blewett, Reverend David Brown, Reverend H.M. Butcher, Reverend Maxwell Cooper, M.M. Crane-Williams, Dr. James Cruickshank, Sue Cruickshank, Reverend Luis Curran, Reverend Grant Dale, Reverend W.C. Daniel, Reverend Don Dodman, Theo Du Moulin, Irene Eaglestone, Reverend E.D. Eldridge, Reverend Patrick Ellis, Mrs. Lacey Evans, Bertha Farquhar, Margaret Foster, Reverend A. Godwin, Reverend J. Godwin, Marion Grove, May Gutteridge, Canon T.E. Harris, Ena C. Harrold, Dr. Hilda Hellaby, Reverend Art Hives, Harriet Holmes, Diane Jeffries, Mrs. M. Korbie, Bruce Korstrom, Wilma McLachlan, Betty McQuillan, Reverend Jack Major, the Matador Motor Inn (Moose Jaw), Reverend Dennis Morgan, Canon Gordon Nakayama, Alice and Frank Neale, Reverend A.A.T. Northrup, Reverend J.D. Parker, Mrs. E. Pellant, Joyce Perry, Daniel Powers, Edith Powis, Selwyn Rocksborough-Smith, Reverend E.J. Rockwood, Roland St. Cyr, Kathleen Scott, Dorothy Sullivan, Reverend Fred Thirkell, Grace Tucker, Reverend Cyril Venables, Lucy M. Wade, Mrs. Jane Barker Wright, Mrs. V.F. Wright and Reverend W.A. Youngman.

Among the sources to which I am greatly indebted are *Pioneer Church Work in British Columbia* by Herbert H. Gowen; *The Anglican Church in British Columbia* by Frank A. Peake; *The Anglican Church in Canada* by Philip Carrington; *Early days in British Columbia* and *Pioneer Days in British Columbia* by Violet E. Sillitoe; *A Bishop in the Rough* by John Sheepshanks; *Father Pat, A Hero of the Far West* by Mrs. Jerome Mercier; *History of British Columbia* by Alexander Begg; *Memoirs of a Cathedral* by Leslie Pearson; *The First Fifty Years* by Marjorie Allan; *Our Story* by Mrs. Willoughby Cummings; *Vancouver: Milltown to Metropolis* by Alan Morley; *Vancouver's First Century* by the staff of *Urban Reader;British Columbia: The Pioneer Years* by T.W. Paterson; *The Man for a New Country* by David R. Williams; *New Westminster: The Early Years* by Alan Woodland; *The Days of My Sojourning* by Cecil Swanson; *In the Sea of Sterile*

Mountains by James Morton; "Anglican Missions to the Japanese in Canada" by Timothy M. Nakayama in the *Journal of the Canadian Church Historical Society*, June 1966; *Via Media* 1960-61, edited by E.S. Gale, *Unity in Diversity* (thesis in VST Archives) by Mary Doris Burton; *Man of the Sea* by Marion Antle Mennes; John Antle's memoirs (manuscript in VST Archives); "John Antle" by Honor M. Kidd in the *Canadian Medical Association Journal,* 1951; the files of James Andrew Bigg; "The View from the Martello Tower" by Steve Cummings in the *West End Courier*, December 9, 1975; articles in the *Vancouver Sun* and the *Vancouver Province*, in particular many by Martha Robinson, Bill Dunford, and Mary McAlpine; and various parish histories and church reports and publications, including *Canadian Churchman* (especially "Random Thoughts by Rex" and O.R Rowley's episcopal profiles), *Across the Rockies, Anglican News* and *Topic* (especially, in addition to articles cited in the text, "The Woman Priest: A Growing Reality" by Deborah Hodge, January, 1978; "The View from Epiphany Chapel" by Maureen Korman, November-December, 1977; "The Church, the Banks and South Africa" by Cynthia Llewellyn, Easter, 1978; and "Helping the Church to Think Again" by Robert Ross, Lent, 1978).

Lyndon Grove
August, 1979

Credits for Pictorial Materials:

Anglican Archives, VST 6, 20a, 21, 23b, 24, 25a, 26, 30, 31, 32, 40, 42, 48, 52, 56, 61, 64, 74a, 75, 76, 77, 82, 84, 88, 89, 90, 91, 92, 95, 96a, 96b, 97, 101, 102, 103, 104, 105, 106, 107b, 107c, 111, 112a, 112b, 113, 130, 133, 134a, 138, 153, 155, 170, 194.
Anglican Church Women, Diocese of New Westminster 65, 145.
British Columbia Provincial Archives 16a.
Christ Church Cathedral 93, 99.
Foster, Margaret 115, 121, 122, 123, 124, 180a
Flying Angel Missions to Seamen 107a, 182a, 182b, 182c.
Gower, Most Reverend Godfrey P. 127, 134b, 136, 141, 142, 146, 147, 179, 200a
Harrison, The Rev. Ronald, and Diocesan Papers (*Anglican News, Topic*) 1, 8, 12, 108a, 110b, 128, 137, 143, 144, 148, 150, 156, 157, 158, 159, 160, 161, 162, 163, 164, 166, 168, 169, 172, 173, 174, 178, 180b, 183, 184a, 184b, 185, 186, 187, 188, 190, 191a, 192, 193, 196.
Hellaby, Hilda 94, 116, 119.
MacQuillan, Betty 83
Mennes, Marion Antle 74b.
New Westminster, Public Library 14, 15a, 20b, 49, 100.
Powell, The Rev. Eric 140, 175.
Sullivan, Dorothy 108b, 109.
Vancouver City Archives 16b, 17, 18, 22a, 22b, 23a, 25b, 27, 28, 29, 36, 38, 47a, 47b, 58, 66, 70, 71, 73, 80, 81, 126.
Vancouver Public Library 15b, 19, 33, 34, 35, 37, 39, 40, 44, 46, 51, 54, 55, 60, 68, 78, 110a, 118, 120.
Wade, Lucy M. 98a, 98b
Wright, James R. 62, 176, 177, 200b.
Anglican Church Women, Diocese of New Westminster 65, 145.

Index

Index

DIOCESE OF NEW WESTMINSTER

"Hallowed this dwelling where the Lord abideth,
This is none other than the gate of heaven;
Strangers and pilgrims, seeking homes eternal,
Pass through its portals." (Camp Artaban chapel.)